W9-BXW-358

PRACTICE

MAKES

PERFECT

SPANISH PRONOUNS AND PREPOSITIONS

Dorothy Richmond

PASSPORT BOOKS
a division of NTC/Contemporary Publishing Company
Lincolnwood, Illinois USA

To Daisy Astrid Richmond

Editorial Director: Cindy Krejcsi
Executive Editor: Mary Jane Maples
Editor: Elizabeth Millán
Director, World Languages Publishing: Keith Fry
Design Manager: Ophelia M. Chambliss
Production Manager: Margo Goia
Production Coordinator: Denise M. Duffy

ISBN: 0-8442-7311-2

Published by Passport Books,
a division of NTC/Contemporary Publishing Company,
4255 West Touhy Avenue,
Lincolnwood (Chicago), Illinois 60646-1975 U.S.A.
© 1998 NTC/Contemporary Publishing Company

Library of Congress Catalog Card Number: 97-69977

7890 CU 0987654321

Table of Contents

Acknowledgments

If necessity is the mother of invention, then academic frustration is the mother of textbook writing. This was the case when a former University of St. Thomas student, Frank Merrill, requested repeatedly more worksheets, more materials, more of anything on pronouns. Frank was not the first student to make such a request, but he was the most persistent, and these continued requests became the inspiration for this book. In trying to provide Frank with what he wanted and needed—a book on pronouns—I discovered that it didn't exist. And so I decided, out of my own frustration, to write one. Thank you, Frank. While students can be the inspiration for a book, they can also be great editors in that they, ultimately, determine if a text works—that is, if it makes sense and teaches. Lisa Nilles, Curt Roy, and John Hering, three of my private students, worked through several manuscript chapters of this book, each offering suggestions and candid comments with regard to clarity, completeness, and content. They were also great at catching typos. Susana Blanco Iglesias, who has worked with me on other projects, then proofread the final manuscript, a job that few people are capable of taking on, but one which Susana always handles with both gusto and grace, making this difficult and challenging task both enjoyable and a great learning experience. Next, Joe Thurston, my technological savior, who has helped me with all my books, prepared the manuscript in its final disc form for publication. Without Joe's help, I still might be writing on a typewriter, perhaps even with a quill. At NTC/Contemporary Publishing Company, Elizabeth Millán, Foreign Language Editor in the Education Division, worked with the text and me from its inception to delivery of manuscript. Elizabeth was greatly supportive of the project and enormously helpful with regard to both form and content. It was at Elizabeth's urging that I included the section on prepositions. I am very fortunate to work for a second time on a book with Elizabeth. And thanks go every day to and for my husband Martin, whose presence improves and adds joy to all aspects of my life.

Dorothy Richmond

Preface

Pronouns and prepositions are two aspects of language study that often fall through the cracks. It is not unusual to encounter individuals who have studied Spanish for years and whose vocabulary and ability to conjugate verbs are impressive, yet they trip over pronouns, unable to distinguish between a direct and an indirect object pronoun, and they still really don't "get" *para* and *por.*

To say that Spanish pronouns and prepositions are undertaught and underlearned is an understatement. Though vastly different on the surface, the mastery of both requires meticulous attention to detail, careful study of both vocabulary and theory, and what often seems like endless, repetitive practice and use, until that magic moment when one simply uses these terms, without thought, without effort, without regret for the time and energy spent learning them.

Current books on the market invariably fall short of providing sufficient material and exercises and allowing the student to learn properly how to work with Spanish pronouns and prepositions. *Practice Makes Perfect: Spanish Pronouns and Prepositions* meets the need for explaining and practicing these two vital parts of speech. Mastery of pronouns and prepositions is essential for all students who desire to communicate with native speakers of Spanish or who simply wish to absorb the wealth of literature, from the classics to the latest fan magazines, in Spanish.

The challenge of this text, for both the author and the student, is to take on these two highly important, yet often ignored, aspects of the Spanish language. For every student who takes this challenge, I offer you congratulations and wish you great academic fortune.

Dorothy Richmond

Introduction

In order to work with anything—a software program, a car, or a language—one must know its constituent parts, their labels, and how to use them. This book deals primarily with pronouns and prepositions; however, these terms, standing alone, are meaningless.

What Is a Pronoun?

A pronoun replaces an understood noun. Therefore, in order to use a pronoun, the speaker/writer and listener/reader must already be in agreement on the meaning of a noun. If you breeze into a room and announce, "I saw him last night," you will be greeted by blank stares and the question "Whom did you see?" On the other hand, if you made this same announcement after you and your friends had been talking about the ghost of Elvis, you still might get some stares, but everyone would understand you. And being understood—putting what is going on in your mind into someone else's mind—is the essence and the aim of all communication.

Pronouns allow us to streamline our conversations, make them less wordy, more interesting. As you begin to work with Spanish pronouns, you may at times find them frustrating, even overwhelming. Keep going. They take time to learn, and other books currently on the market do not give them their due credit; nor do these texts offer and allow students sufficient explanations, examples, and exercises.

Part I of *Practice Makes Perfect: Spanish Pronouns and Prepositions* offers you fourteen units about pronouns in Spanish, from the everyday subject pronoun to the specialized reciprocal pronoun. Each unit contains an abundance of explanations, examples, and exercises. (At the back of the book you'll find answers to all the exercises.)

What Is a Preposition?

A preposition reveals a relationship. Prepositions show place, time, direction, manner, and companionship. Often, this relationship is between two nouns or pronouns; however, prepositions can also show a relationship between a noun and a verb (the preposition then, technically, becomes an adverb).

It is difficult to speak or write very long without using a preposition. It is even harder to "fake it," when you don't know the name for the preposition you want. Unlike nouns and verbs, which often have synonyms or which you can describe in other terms or even just point to or demonstrate "à la charades," prepositions are what they are, and it is crucial to know them in order to get your point across.

Imagine trying to say "John lives with Matt" if you don't know the word for "with." Or, "I have a gift for Daisy," if you don't know how to say "for." "To the right of," "to the left of," "in front of," and so on—all these terms are what they are and need to be learned and mastered in order to be a confident, comfortable speaker of any language.

Prepositions are brought out in all their glory and forms in the three units in Part II of this text. In the first unit, you are presented with the basic vocabulary, various uses, and at times subtle differences among certain prepositions that initially may appear to be interchangeable. The second unit is devoted solely to *para* and *por,* two prepositions with frequently similar meanings, but distinct uses. Finally, in the third unit, you will learn about the special relationship that many prepositions have with verbs.

Each unit in Part II of *Practice Makes Perfect: Spanish Pronouns and Prepositions* contains detailed explanations of the material covered, followed by examples and exercises. (Answers to these exercises, too, can be found at the end of the text.)

The appendices in Part III consist of valuable charts and concise explanations and summaries. For example, "The Eight Parts of Speech," two of which are the pronoun and the preposition, arm you with the terms you will need to understand references in this text, as well as give you the ability to identify all eight parts of speech when working with the language. Next, you'll find concise summaries that serve as reference tools in "Pronoun Definitions and Charts" and "Prepositions."

Finally, as I've already mentioned, there is an Answer Key section that contains the answers for all the numbered exercises in the text.

I sincerely wish that this text will help those who study Spanish, at any level, to achieve (and maybe surpass?) their goals of speaking, writing, and reading this incredibly rich language with greater competence and confidence. Enjoy the language. Play with it. Work with it. Make it a part of you. *¡Buena suerte!*

Dorothy Richmond

NISH PRONOUNS & PREPOSITION
        5107761 QP T   7.96
    9.95 20%TEACHER
NISH VERB TENSES
        1482661 QP T   7.96
    9.95 20%TEACHER
IT TO GRANDMA W/CAS-SPAN
        4831093 MU T   13.56
    16.95 20%TEACHER
CUAN LEJOS LLEGARAS
        5830952 CL T   12.76
    15.95 20%TEACHER
DA MARIA-SPANISH
        4826736 QP T   4.80
    6.00 20%TEACHER
ORO Y ESMERALDAS
        5480165 QP T   5.59
    6.99 20%TEACHER
SPANISH NOW-LEVEL 2 E2
        1615869 TA T   14.96
    19.95 25% COUPON

        Subtotal   67.59
        MARYLAND 5%   3.38
        Total   70.97
        MASTERCARD   70.97
/K 5401260941008
            AUTH: 035589

CUSTOMER COPY

04/12/1999 04:53PM

Subject Pronouns

Subject (or Personal) Pronouns

In English there are seven subject pronouns (also called personal pronouns): *I, you, he, she, it, we, they*. In Spanish, however, the pronoun also agrees with the gender of its subject, giving us a greater selection from which to choose.

Singular	Plural
yo (I)	**nosotros** (we—masc./masc. & fem.) **nosotras** (we—fem. only)
tú (you—familiar)	**vosotros** (you—familiar; masc./ masc. & fem.) **vosotras** (you—familiar; fem. only)
él (he) **ella** (she) **usted** (you—formal)	**ellos** (they—masc./masc. & fem.) **ellas** (they—fem. only) **ustedes** (you—formal)

Notes:

1. The pronouns **usted** and **ustedes** are often abbreviated in texts. **Ud.** or **Vd.** is used for **usted; Uds.** or **Vds.** is used for **ustedes.**

2. The familiar plural **vosotros** form is used primarily in Peninsular Spanish (i.e., Spain), while throughout Latin America **ustedes** is used in both formal and familiar situations.

The subject pronoun reveals who or what the agent or actor is in a sentence. The conjugated verb must agree with this subject. The Spanish regular verb endings are given below. Use the verb-ending chart to match with the preceding chart for subject pronouns. This will help you do the first exercise.

-ar		-er		-ir	
o	amos	o	emos	o	imos
as	áis	es	éis	es	ís
a	an	e	en	e	en

ejercicio   I-1-1

Write the appropriate subject pronoun before each conjugated verb below. The verbs involved all are regular -ar, -er, and -ir verbs.

1. _____ hablo

2. _____ comemos

3. _____ viven

4. _____ canta

5. _____ abrís

6. _____ vendemos

7. _____ escribe

8. _____ describen

9. _____ practicáis

10. _____ estudias

11. _____ ama

12. _____ sufro

13. _____ bebes

14. _____ tomáis

15. _____ lee

16. _____ creo

17. _____ llegas

18. _____ comprendemos

19. _____ trabajan

20. _____ miras

Notes:

1. It is often not necessary even to state or write the subject pronoun. (In English we must include the subject pronoun with the verb.) In Spanish it is only necessary to include the subject pronoun for one of the following reasons:

   a. *Clarity.* This occurs usually in the third person, allowing you to differentiate between **él** and **ella** or **ellos** and **ustedes,** for example.

   b. *Emphasis.* When you want to mark the difference between two subjects, even though they are understood, you can bring in the subject pronoun:

   ¡**Yo** vivo en una casa, pero **tú** vives en un palacio!
   I live in a house, but *you* live in a palace!

2. There is no Spanish word for the subject pronoun *it*. When *it* (or its plural *they*) is the subject of a sentence or phrase, *it* (or *they*) is understood:

¿De qué color es tu casa?	**Es** blanca.
What color is your house?	*It is* white.
¿Dónde están los coches?	**Están** en el garaje.
Where are the cars?	*They are* in the garage.

ejercicio   I-1-2

Fill in each blank with the appropriate subject pronoun or verb ending, according to the information given. The verbs below all are commonly used irregular verbs.

1. _____ tengo

2. _____ tienes

3. él quier _____

4. nosotros est _____

5. vosotros sal _____

6. _____ quieren

7. yo pued _____

8. ella vien _____

9. _____ somos

10. tú sal _____

11. usted jueg _____

12. _____ pongo

13. ustedes pon _____

14. ellos dic _____

15. _____ estáis

16. _____ oyes

17. ellas pued _____

18. nosotros ve _____

19. _____ oímos

20. _____ veis

Interrogative Pronouns

The interrogative pronoun is used to ask a specific type of question. The answer sought will be a noun (either a thing or the name of a person). *Who* is in the soundproof booth? *To whom* did you send the poison pen letter? *Whose* dog did this? *What* is this? *Which* do you prefer? These interrogatives elicit nouns (or pronouns) for answers.

¿Quién? ¿Quiénes?	Who?
¿A quién? ¿A quiénes?	(To) Whom?
¿De quién? ¿De quiénes?	Whose?
¿Qué?	What? (Which?)
¿Cuál? ¿Cuáles?	Which? (What?)

Note: In Spanish, **¿Qué?** often precedes a noun and **¿Cuál?** often precedes a verb or a prepositional phrase.

Also note that all the Spanish interrogative pronouns, with the exception of **¿Qué?** have a singular and a plural form. The verb must agree in number with this form.

Who?: *¿Quién? ¿Quiénes?*

When your question is about one or more people and the answer you seek involves a name or names, you use *Who?*, as in *Who* has the cat? John has the cat. (John is the subject of the answer.) In these cases in Spanish, you will use either **¿Quién?** or **¿Quiénes?** (when you are seeking the names of more than one person).

examples:

subject (*s.*)	**¿Quién** vive aquí? Pedro Morales vive aquí.
	Who lives here? Pedro Morales lives here.
subject (*pl.*)	**¿Quiénes** trabajan aquí? Pedro y Felipe trabajan aquí.
	Who works here? Pedro and Felipe work here.
with **ser** (*s.*)	**¿Quién** es él? Él es Pedro Morales.
	Who is he? He is Pedro Morales.
with **ser** (*pl.*)	**¿Quiénes** son ellos? Ellos son los carpinteros.
	Who are they? They are the carpenters.

ejercicio I-2-1

Translate the following questions.

1. Who is she? _____

2. Who are they (*m.*)? _____

3. Who are you (*s.*)? _____

4. Who are you (*pl.*)? _____

5. Who works here? _____

6. Who watches the television? _____

7. Who speaks Spanish here? _____

8. Who doesn't live here? _____

9. Who writes the book? _____

10. Who is your friend? _____

Whom?: *¿A quién? ¿A quiénes?*

When you want to know the name of the person who is the recipient of an action (object of the verb), you use *Whom?*, as in *Whom* do you love? (direct object) or *To whom* are you writing? (indirect object). In Spanish, these situations require that you add **a** before the interrogative **¿quién?** or **¿quiénes?** (if you suspect that the answer will involve more than one name).

examples:

direct object　　**¿A quién** ves? Veo a Pedro Morales.
　　　　　　　　Whom do you see? I see Pedro Morales.
indirect object　**¿A quiénes** escribes? Escribo a Pedro y a Manolo.
　　　　　　　　To whom are you writing? I'm writing to Pedro and to Manolo.

When the referent is a direct object, that **a** will be the personal **a**. When the referent is an indirect object, that **a** will represent the English preposition *to* or *at*.

Note: You will not use the personal **a** with the verbs **ser, estar,** and **tener.**

ejercicio I-2-2

For the following translations, use the second-person singular form of the present-tense verb.

1. Whom do you love? _____

2. Whom do you see (*ver*)? _____

3. Whom (*s.*) are you watching (*mirar*)? _____

4. Whom (*pl.*) are you watching? _____

5. For whom (*s.*) are you looking (*buscar*)? _____

6. For whom (*pl.*) are you looking? _____

7. To whom (*s.*) do you listen? _____

8. To whom (*pl.*) do you listen? _____

9. Whom (*s.*) do you know (*conocer*)? _____

10. Whom (*pl.*) do you know? _____

Whose?: ¿De quién? ¿De quiénes?

When you want to know who the owner(s) is (are) of something, you will use the phrase **¿De quién?** or **¿De quiénes?** In simple questions, the phrase, usually followed by a form of **ser,** is uncomplicated:

¿De quién es este libro?   **¿De quiénes** son esos boletos?
Whose book is this?   *Whose* tickets are those?

However, the use of the phrase does not translate directly in more complicated questions, and it becomes necessary to rephrase the question. For example, *Whose grandmother lives here?* becomes **¿La abuela de quién vive aquí?**

¿De quién son los vecinos que no hablan inglés?
Whose neighbors don't speak English?
(Literally: *Of whom* are the neighbors that don't speak English?)

¿De quién era el lápiz que pediste prestado?
Whose pencil did you borrow?
(Literally: *Of whom* was the pencil that you borrowed?)

¿De quiénes son los sombreros que están en la mesa?
Whose hats are on the table?
(Literally: *Of whom* are the hats that are on the table?)

¿De quiénes son los videos más populares ahora?
Whose videos are the most popular now?
(Literally: *Of whom* are the most popular videos now?)

ejercicio   I-2-3

The Spanish syntax is given in parentheses to the right.

1. Whose car is this? (Of whom is this car?)

_____

2. Whose keys (*la llave*) are on the table? (Of whom are the keys that are on the table?)

_____

3. Whose (*pl.*) cars are dirty? (Of whom are the cars that are dirty?)

_____

4. Whose (*pl.*) children (*f.*) are reading these books? (Of whom are the children that are reading these books?)

_____

5. Whose cat is drinking (*beber*) the milk? (Of whom is the cat that is drinking the milk?)

_____

6. Whose neighbors (*el vecino*) live in the blue house? (Of whom are the neighbors that live in the blue house?)

_____

7. Whose (*pl.*) students are the most intelligent? (Of whom are the most intelligent students?)

_____

8. Whose car doesn't run (*funcionar*)? (Of whom is the car that doesn't run?)

_____

9. Whose coat is this? (Of whom is this coat?)

_____

10. Whose parrot (*el loro*) speaks Italian? (Of whom is the parrot that speaks Italian?)

_____

11. Whose (*pl.*) cassettes (*el casete*) are these? (Of whom are these cassettes?)

_____

12. Whose backpack (*la mochila*) is that? (Of whom is that backpack?)

_____

Which?: *¿Qué? ¿Cuál? ¿Cuáles?*

When you want to limit a group of items or when you want someone to make a choice among a number of items, you will ask *Which?* or *What?* In English, *Which?* generally precedes a noun (Which book do you want?), while the limiting *What?* usually precedes a verb (What is the best book?).

In Spanish, the opposite is usually true. If the word following the interrogative pronoun is a noun, use **¿Qué?** If the word following the interrogative pronoun is a verb or a prepositional phrase, use **¿Cuál?** (or **¿Cuáles?**). In the context of **¿Cuál?** + verb, **¿Cuál?** usually means "Which one?"

examples:

¿Qué vestido prefieres? Prefiero el vestido largo.
Which dress do you prefer? I prefer the long dress.

¿Cuál prefieres? Prefiero el vestido largo.
Which one do you prefer? I prefer the long dress.

¿Cuál de los vestidos prefieres? Prefiero el vestido rojo.
Which of the dresses do you prefer? I prefer the red dress.

¿Cuáles prefieres? Prefiero los zapatos negros.
Which ones do you prefer? I prefer the black shoes.

¿Cuál de las pinturas es de Miró?
Which (one) of the paintings is by Miró?

¿Qué pintura es de Miró?
Which painting is by Miró?

¿Cuál es tu número de teléfono? Mi número es 555-1212.
Which one [of the millions out there] is your telephone number? My number is 555-1212.

¿Qué número de teléfono es correcto?
Which telephone number is correct?

ejercicio   I-2-4

Remember: Which? + noun, use **¿Qué?**; *Which? + verb, use* **¿Cuál(es)?**; *Which? + prepositional phrase, use* **¿Cuál(es)?** *Also use you =* **tú** *or* **tu.**

1. Which book is more (*más*) interesting? _____

2. Which actor is more popular? _____

3. Which girl (*la chica*) is your cousin? _____

4. Which food has more fat (*la grasa*)? _____

5. Which store sells more clothing? _____

6. Which do you eat more, chicken (*el pollo*) or fish (*el pescado*)? _____

7. Which is more popular? _____

8. What (*Which*) is your name? _____

9. What (*Which*) is your address (*la dirección*)? _____

10. Which ones do you wear more? _____

11. Which shoes do you wear more? _____

12. Which hat is more comfortable (*cómodo*)? _____

13. Which of the hats is more comfortable? _____

14. Which program (*el programa*) do you watch? _____

15. Which (*pl.*) of the new programs do you watch? _____

16. Which ones do you watch? _____

¿Qué? versus *¿Cuál?*: What's Really Going On?

Whether to use **¿Qué?** or **¿Cuál?** in questions confounds many speakers of English. In a nutshell, questions beginning with **¿Qué?** are trying to elicit a definition, whereas questions that begin with **¿Cuál?** ask the respondent to limit his or her answer to one of a possible many. Consider the following questions and their literal implications as displayed in the answers:

¿Qué es tu nombre? Mi nombre es la palabra que la gente usa cuando me llama.
What is your name? My name is the word that people use when they call to me.

¿Cuál es tu nombre? Mi nombre es Penelope.
What is your name? (Which is your name from the world of names?) My name is Penelope.

As you can see, **¿Qué?** requests a literal answer, and **¿Cuál?** asks for a selection from a large pool of possible answers.

To determine if you will use **¿Qué?** or **¿Cuál?**, consider the following:

1. As stated in the preceding section, generally speaking, **¿Qué?** will precede a noun, and **¿Cuál?** will precede a verb.

2. Beyond that, ask yourself what it is that you want. If you want a definition, use **¿Qué?** If there are many possible answers and you want to know the true one(s) in a particular situation—that is, the limited answer(s)—use **¿Cuál?**

ejercicio   I-2-5

Decide whether you would use ¿Qué? or ¿Cuál? in the following questions. Then translate the questions.

	¿Qué?	¿Cuál?
1. What day is today?	_____	_____
2. What is the date (*la fecha*) today?	_____	_____

	¿Qué?	¿Cuál?
3. What is his name?	———	———
4. What time (*la hora*) is it?	———	———
5. What is your reason (*la razón*) for this (*esto*)?	———	———
6. What is that (*eso*)?	———	———
7. Which book do you want?	———	———
8. Which ones do you want?	———	———
9. Which woman is your friend?	———	———
10. What does this mean (*significar*)?	———	———
11. What is the answer (*la respuesta*)?	———	———
12. What do you want to know (*saber*)?	———	———

Pronouns as Objects of Prepositions

FUNCTION: Replace the name of a person or thing following a preposition (e.g., for, from, with, etc.)

SPANISH PLACEMENT: Immediately following a preposition

ENGLISH EQUIVALENTS: me, you, him, her, it, us, them

The Standard Prepositional Object Pronoun

The pronouns that follow prepositions are nearly identical to the subject pronouns. The only change comes with the first- and second-person singular forms: **mí** and **ti.** Note that in this context **mí** takes an accent over the *i* to distinguish it from **mi,** the possessive adjective, which means "my."

Singular	Plural
mí (me)	**nosotros** (us—masc./masc. & fem.) **nosotras** (us—fem. only)
ti (you—familiar)	**vosotros** (you—familiar; masc./ masc. & fem.) **vosotras** (you—familiar; fem. only)
él (him) **ella** (her; it, fem.) **usted** (you—formal) **ello** (it, m.; neut.)	**ellos** (them; it) **ellas** (them; it) **ustedes** (you—formal)

After a preposition, the word **ello** means "it" when the referent is an object, event, or idea that is masculine or neuter; use **ella** for a feminine referent.

El accidente sucedió hace un año. Él escribió un cuento acerca de **ello.**
The accident happened a year ago. He wrote a story about *it.*

Compramos una cama nueva y tenemos las almohadas perfectas para **ella.**
We're buying a new bed, and we have the perfect pillows for *it.*

In the following exercise, you will be working with a few commonly used prepositions. For a fuller discussion and more complete vocabulary listing of prepositions, consult Part II of this text.

ejercicio   I-3-1

Use the following prepositions to translate the sentences. Unless otherwise indicated, you = the second-person singular familiar form (tú).

vocabulario

about	**acerca de**	near	**cerca de**
behind	**detrás de**	on top of	**encima de**
for	**para**	to the left of	**a la izquierda de**
from; of	**de**	to the right of	**a la derecha de**
in front of	**delante de**	underneath	**debajo de**

1. He has a book for me. _____

2. I have a gift for you. _____

3. What do you have for me? _____

4. The table is from her. _____

5. I buy my books from them. _____

6. He is in front of it (*m.*). _____

7. You are behind him. _____

8. He lives near me. _____

9. The carpet (*la alfombra*) is underneath us (*f.*). _____

10. He lives near you (*pl.*). _____

11. He writes a book about her. _____

12. We walk behind them. _____

13. She dances to the right of me. _____

14. They work to the left of you. _____

15. The food is in front of us. _____

Pronouns with *con*

Certain pronouns following the preposition **con** (with) undergo some changes. They are as follows:

Singular	Plural
conmigo (with me)	**con nosotros/as** (with us)
contigo (with you)	**con vosotros/as** (with you)
consigo (with him; with her; with you)	**consigo** (with them; with you)
or	or
con él (with him)	**con ellos** (with them)
con ella (with her, it)	**con ellas** (with them)
con usted (with you)	**con ustedes** (with you)
con ello (with it)	

Notes:

1. In the first- and second-person singular, **mí** and **ti** become **conmigo** and **contigo**.

   ¿Por qué no vienes **conmigo** al concierto?   Está bien. Iré **contigo**.
   Why don't you come *with me* to the concert?   OK. I'll go *with you*.

2. In the third person, whether singular or plural, you usually use **consigo** when the prepositional pronoun is referring to the subject pronoun. You use **con** plus the appropriate pronoun when the prepositional pronoun refers to someone other than the subject of the sentence.

   Él llevó los libros **consigo.**
   He took the books *with him.*

   Mi hermano vive en San Diego y mi padre vive **con él.**
   My brother lives in San Diego, and my father lives *with him.*

3. In the **nosotros** and **vosotros** forms, there is no change between the subject pronoun and that following the prepositions.

ejercicio   I-3-2

Use the clues in parentheses to determine the appropriate form of you.

1. I'm with you (*s., fam.*). _____

2. You (*s., formal*) are with me. _____

3. She's with him. _____

4. He's with her. _____

5. I work with you (*s., fam.*) now. _____

6. They live with me. _____

7. Does she study with you (*s., fam.*)? _____

8. Who lives with you (*pl., formal*)? _____

9. Why don't you (*s., fam.*) dance with him? _____

10. I want to speak with you (*s., formal*). _____

11. He lives with us. _____

12. She always takes the keys (*la llave*) with her. _____

13. They (*m.*) never take the keys with them. _____

14. Martin is with me. _____

15. Why don't you (*s., formal*) take the umbrella (*el paraguas*) with you? _____

_____

16. Why don't they (*f.*) take the umbrella with them? _____

The Six Exceptions

There are six prepositions that take a subject pronoun, rather than the object pronouns discussed in this unit. These six exceptions are as follows:

entre	between	**excepto***	except
incluso	including	**menos***	except
según	according to	**salvo***	except

_____

*The three prepositions *excepto, menos,* and *salvo,* all of which mean "except," for the most part can be used interchangeably.

examples:

Juan está **entre tú y yo.**
Juan is *between you and me.*

Según él, debemos llegar pronto.
According to him, we should be there soon.

Todos bailan **excepto (menos, salvo) él.**
Everyone dances, *except him.*

Todos vamos a la fiesta, **incluso tú.**
We're all going to the party, *including you.*

ejercicio   I-3-3

Unless otherwise indicated, you = second-person singular.

1. There are twenty people here, including you and me.

_____

2. According to her, money can buy happiness (*la felicidad*).

_____

3. Between you, me, and the grand piano (*el piano de cola*), this painting is ghastly (*espantoso*).

_____

4. I think (*creer*) that everybody (*todo el mundo*) speaks French here, except me.

_____

5. Between us and them, we have enough (*suficiente*) money.

_____

6. Everyone (*todos*) here is outraged (*escandalizado*), including me.

_____

7. Everyone in the neighborhood (*la vecindad*) has a swimming pool (*la piscina*), except us.

_____

8. We are in a lot of trouble (*tener muchas dificultades*), according to me.

_____

9. Everybody is ready (*listo*), except you (*s., formal*).

_____

10. According to them, it is possible to live on Mars (*Marte*).

_____

Reflexive Pronouns Following a Preposition

When you do something for yourself, it is called a reflexive action because the action goes directly back to the actor. (For a more complete discussion of reflexive pronouns, see Unit 11.) Expressing a reflexive action can be done in two ways, with a reflexive pronoun alone or with a preposition. If you choose to use the preposition, then the pronouns that follow it will be:

a mí mismo	to myself	**a nosotros mismos**	to ourselves
a mí misma	to myself	**a nosotras mismas**	to ourselves
a ti mismo	to yourself	**a vosotros mismos**	to yourselves
a ti misma	to yourself	**a vosotras mismas**	to yourselves
a sí mismo/a	to himself/herself, ourself, itself	**a sí mismos/as**	to themselves, yourselves

examples:

Preparo el café **para mí mismo.**   Marta, tú piensas solamente **en ti misma.**
I prepare the coffee *for myself.*   Marta, you think only *about yourself.*

Los buenos maestros enseñan **a sí mismos** también.
Good teachers teach *themselves* too.

ejercicio   I-3-4

1. I buy the car for (*para*) myself. _____

2. He does everything for (*para*) himself. _____

3. They do everything by (*por*) themselves. _____

4. She hurts (*perjudicar a*) herself when she tells a lie (*la mentira*). _____

_____

5. You (*pl., fam.*) only (*sólo*) hurt yourselves. _____

6. I write notes (*la nota*) to myself in order to (*para*) remember (*recordar*) the things that I need to do.

_____

7. You should have time for (*para*) yourself every day. _____

_____

8. She always buys a gift for herself on her birthday. _____

_____

9. When I travel, I send my purchases (*la compra*) to myself through the mail (*por correo*).

_____

10. You (*s., formal*) can't sell your house to (*a*) yourself. It's ridiculous! _____

_____

traducción   I-3-5

Pedro is my friend. I am very happy because he lives next door to me. A raccoon lives underneath my house. Between you (*pl.*) and me, I think (*believe*) that raccoons are interesting animals. I'm reading a book about them now. Usually the raccoon lives in a tree, but I am lucky because my house is on top of this raccoon. According to Pedro, the raccoon is part of the bear family, and he believes that if he sees the animal in front of him, it's good-bye, world. When Pedro leaves (*from*) or enters (*into*) my house, he always looks to the left and then to the right.

vocabulario

about	**acerca de**	next door to	**al lado de**
bear	**el oso**	now	**ahora**
(to) enter into	**entrar en**	raccoon	**el mapache**
if	**si**	then	**después**
in front of	**delante de**	tree	**el árbol**
(to) leave from	**salir de**	usually	**usualmente**
(to) be lucky	**tener suerte**	world	**el mundo**

Possessive Pronouns

Possessive pronouns in Spanish are not used as frequently as they are in English. Since these pronouns stand for the owner as well as the object owned, they agree with the object owned in number and gender.

Singular	Plural
mío(s) (mine) **mía(s)** (mine)	**nuestro(s)** (ours) **nuestra(s)** (ours)
tuyo(s) (yours) **tuya(s)** (yours)	**vuestro(s)** (yours) **vuestra(s)** (yours)
suyo(s) (his; hers; yours; its) **suya(s)** (his; hers; yours; its)	**suyo(s)** (theirs; yours) **suya(s)** (theirs; yours)

The possessive pronoun differs from the possessive adjective in that the adjective modifies (and precedes) the noun: **Es mi gato** (It is my cat); whereas the pronoun includes the significance of the noun: **Es mío** (It is mine). The Spanish possessive adjective always precedes a noun. If the noun is plural, then so is the possessive adjective: **mi gato; mis gatos; tu televisor; tus televisores.** The following chart displays the possessive adjectives.

Singular	Plural
mi(s) (my) **tu(s)** (your) **su(s)** (his; her; your; its)	**nuestro/a(s)** (our) **vuestro/a(s)** (your) **su(s)** (their; your)

Possessive Pronouns Following *ser*

The possessive pronoun frequently is found following the third-person conjugations of **ser**—namely, **es** and **son.**

¿El chaleco? **Es mío.**   ¿Las herramientas? **Son suyas.**
The vest? *It's mine.*   The tools? *They are theirs.*

ejercicio   I-4-1

Change the following possessive adjectives to the appropriate possessive pronouns.

1. Es mi teléfono.   Es _____.

2. Es tu hamburguesa.   Es _____.

3. Es su refrigerador.   Es _____.

4. Son mis anteojos.   Son _____.

5. Son sus relojes.   Son _____.

6. Es nuestra mesa.   Es _____.

7. Son tus tazas.   Son _____.

8. Son vuestros tenedores.   Son _____.

9. Son sus sillas.   Son _____.

10. Es vuestra lámpara.   Es _____.

11. Son mis sábanas (*sheets*).   Son _____.

12. Son tus fundas (*pillowcases*).   Son _____.

13. Son nuestras colchas (*quilts*).   Son _____.

14. Es su pintura.   Es _____.

15. Son sus computadoras.   Son _____.

ejercicio   I-4-2

Express the following statements using possessive pronouns.

1. The cat is mine. / The cats are mine.

2. The snake (*la culebra*) is yours. / The snakes are yours.

_____

3. The bird (*el pájaro*) is hers. / The birds are hers.

_____

4. The monkey (*el mono*) is his. / The monkeys are his.

_____

5. The giraffe (*la jirafa*) is ours. / The giraffes are ours.

_____

6. The pig (*el cerdo*) is theirs. / The pigs are theirs.

_____

7. The spider (*la araña*) is mine. / The spiders are mine.

_____

8. The horse (*el caballo*) is yours. / The horses are yours.

_____

9. The butterfly (*la mariposa*) is hers. / The butterflies are hers.

_____

10. The elephant (*el elefante*) is ours. / The elephants are ours.

_____

A Friend of Mine

The possessive pronoun alone following a noun is expressed in English by *of* followed by the possessive pronoun (*of mine, of ours, of his*, etc.). In Spanish, there is no need to add **de** (*of*). This use of the possessive pronoun adds emphasis to the owner of the object, whereas the use of the possessive adjective usually emphasizes the object owned.

examples:

La amiga suya es bonita.   **El coche suyo** es un clásico.
The friend of hers is pretty.   *The car of his* (His car) is a classic.

Esos compañeros míos son muy listos.
Those classmates of mine are very clever.

ejercicio I-4-3

In this exercise, you = second-person singular.

1. A friend (*m.*) of mine works here. _____

2. A friend (*f.*) of mine lives here. _____

3. Some friends (*m.*) of mine have a cabin (*la cabaña*) in Canada. _____

_____

4. A friend (*f.*) of his studies Spanish. _____

5. I work with a friend (*f.*) of yours. _____

6. A colleague (*el colega*) of ours speaks German (*alemán*) and Gaelic (*gaélico*). _____

_____

7. They don't want to speak with him because he is an enemy (*el enemigo*) of theirs. _____

_____

8. A friend (*m.*) of yours is a friend of mine. _____

9. Those paintings (*la pintura*) of his are fascinating (*encantador*). _____

_____

10. A cousin (*f.*) of ours is a princess (*la princesa*) in Europe (*Europa*). _____

_____

Possessive Pronouns in Statements of Comparison

In Spanish, when we compare or contrast two or more things, usually we will mention the name of the item once and, after that, use a pronoun. This frequently comes into play with possessive pronouns: My house is red, but *yours* [your house] is white.

In these situations, you will need to include the appropriate definite article along with the possessive pronoun.

examples:

Su casa es roja, pero **la suya** es blanca.
His house is red, but *theirs* is white.

Mi automóvil es francés, pero **el suyo** es italiano.
My automobile is French, but *theirs* is Italian.

Sus marcos son de plata, pero **los míos** son de oro.
Her frames are silver, but mine are gold.

Nuestra marca es barata; **la suya** es cara.
Our brand is cheap; theirs is expensive.

ejercicio   I-4-4

Unless otherwise indicated, you = second-person singular.

1. Their house is dirty (*sucio*), but ours is clean (*limpio*). _____

   _____

2. Her books are in the kitchen, and mine are in the dining room. _____

   _____

3. He keeps (*guardar*) his money in the bank, but I keep mine in the mattress (*el colchón*). _____

   _____

4. His cousins live in Hollywood, and hers live in Seattle. _____

   _____

5. Our dog is a collie (*el perro pastor*), and hers is a poodle (*el perro de lana*). _____

   _____

6. Her jewels (*la joya*) are fake (*la imitación*), but mine are real (*auténtico*). _____

   _____

7. They buy their food in the supermarket (*el supermercado*), but we grow (*cultivar*) ours. _____

   _____

8. His attorney (*el abogado*) works for a big firm (*la firma*). Ours has an office in a basement. _____

   _____

9. It's my life. It isn't yours. _____

10. You (*pl., fam.*) have your problems (*el problema*), and I have mine. _____

   _____

Possessive Pronouns with Regular Comparisons

Regular comparisons involve using **más . . . que** (more . . . than), **menos . . . que** (less . . . than), or **tan . . . como** (as . . . as).

Julia es **más alta que** Diego.   Diego es **tan guapo como** Antonio Banderas.
Julia is *taller than* Diego.   Diego is *as handsome as* Antonio Banderas.

When we compare (or contrast) two equally named things or people that are possessed or owned, the first one is mentioned and the second one usually is replaced by the possessive pronoun, which is preceded by the appropriate definite article.

examples:

Mi amigo es **más alto que el tuyo.**   Mi amiga es **más interesante que la vuestra.**
My friend is *taller than yours.*   My friend is *more interesting than yours.*

Su casa es **menos elegante que la nuestra.**
Their house is *less elegant than ours.*

Su gato no es **tan peludo como el mío.**
His cat isn't *as furry as mine.*

Mi café no está **tan sabroso como el tuyo.**
My coffee isn't *as delicious as yours.*

ejercicio   I-4-5

1. Their house is bigger than mine. _____

2. My house isn't as big as theirs. _____

3. Her clothing is more expensive than mine. _____

4. Your (*pl., fam.*) jewels (*la joya*) are more elegant than ours. _____

   _____

5. Her ferret (*el hurón*) isn't as friendly (*amable*) as ours. _____

   _____

6. His thermos (*el termo*) isn't as full (*lleno*) as mine. _____

   _____

7. María's report (*el reportaje*) is more interesting than his. _____

   _____

8. Juan's car is newer than yours (*s., formal*). _____

9. Her envelopes (*el sobre*) are prettier than mine. I'm going to buy a box (*la caja*). _____

   _____

10. Their hammers (*el martillo*) aren't as heavy (*pesado*) as yours (*s., fam.*). _____

   _____

Possessive Pronouns with Irregular Comparisons

There are four irregular adjectives of comparison:

mejor(es)   better   **mayor(es)**   older
peor(es)   worse   **menor(es)**   younger

The Spanish syntax for sentences with these irregular comparatives is identical to that of English. Note that while these irregular comparatives do not take gender, they do agree in number with the subject of the sentence.

examples:

Mi tortuga es **mejor** que la tuya.   Su gorila es **mayor** que el tuyo.
My turtle is *better* than yours.   His gorilla is *older* than yours.

Sus osos son **peores** que los nuestros.   Mis moscas son **menores** que las tuyas.
His bears are *worse* than ours.   My flies are *younger* than yours.

ejercicio   I-4-6

1. Your (*s., fam.*) car is better than mine. _____

2. Their chairs are better than ours. _____

3. My painting is worse than his. _____

4. Elena's furniture (*los muebles*) is worse than his. _____

5. Your (*s., formal*) friend is older than mine. _____

6. My grandparents are older than yours (*s., fam.*). _____

7. Our son is younger than yours (*pl., fam.*). _____

8. Our goldfish (*la carpa dorada*) are younger than theirs. _____

   _____

9. Julia's paella is better than mine. _____

10. Beethoven's music (*la música*) is better than hers. _____

traducción   I-4-7

I am very upset because Silvia has my ring. She says that it is hers, but I know that it is mine because it has my initials. Silvia is a kleptomaniac. Nothing in her house is hers. Many things are mine. For example, all the paintings are mine, the grandfather clock is mine, the candelabra in the dining room is mine, the washer and dryer are mine, even the food in the refrigerator is mine. What can I do? Perry Mason says that possession is (the) ninety-nine percent of the law. Therefore, everything is hers.

vocabulario

candelabra	**el candelabro**	painting	**la pintura**
dryer	**la secadora**	percent	**el por ciento**
even	**hasta**	possession	**la posesión**
everything	**todo**	refrigerator	**el refrigerador**
grandfather clock	**el reloj de péndulo**	ring	**el anillo**
initials	**las iniciales**	therefore	**por eso**
kleptomaniac	**el/la cleptómano/a**	thing	**la cosa**
law	**la ley**	upset	**disgustado/a**
nothing	**nada**	washer	**la lavadora**

_____

_____

_____

_____

_____

_____

_____

_____

_____

_____

_____

_____

_____

Demonstrative Pronouns

If the pronouns in the following chart look familiar to you, you are probably recalling the demonstrative adjectives. Note that demonstrative adjectives and demonstrative pronouns are identical, except the demonstrative pronouns take an accent mark. Think of it like this: if you drop the noun, the demonstrative adjective picks up an accent mark and becomes a demonstrative pronoun.

The exception to this rule is the neuter forms: **esto, eso,** and **aquello.** These forms will be discussed later.

	Masculine	Feminine	Neuter
this	**éste**	**ésta**	**esto**
these	**éstos**	**éstas**	
that	**ése**	**ésa**	**eso**
those	**ésos**	**ésas**	
that over there	**aquél**	**aquélla**	**aquello**
those over there	**aquéllos**	**aquéllas**	

Demonstrative Pronouns with Gender

When the pronoun refers to and includes the significance of something in particular, the gender and number of that referent will be reflected in the pronoun.

examples:

Este coche es mío, pero **ése** es suyo.
This car is mine, but *that one* is his.

La mejor marca es **ésta.**
The best brand is *this* one.

Estas ventanas están limpias, pero **ésas** todavía faltan por limpiar.
These windows are clean, but *those* still need to be cleaned.

Aquellas mesas son de roble, **ésas** son de pino y **éstas** son de caoba.
Those tables over there are oak, *those* are pine, and *these* are mahogany.

ejercicio   I-5-1

1. This book is mine, but that (*one*) is his. _____

2. This house is pretty, but that (*one*) is prettier. _____

3. These shoes are mine, and those are his. _____

4. These chairs are hers, and those are mine. _____

5. That boy over there is my neighbor (*el vecino*) and this (*boy*) is my son. _____

_____

6. These women are my neighbors, but those (*women*) over there are from some other (*otro*) city.

_____

7. That car is John's (*of John*), and that one over there is mine. _____

_____

8. These magazines are terrible, but these are much better. _____

_____

9. This telephone works (*funcionar*), but that one (*over there*) never works. _____

_____

10. These programs (*el programa*) are terrible, but those are even (*aún*) worse. _____

_____

Neuter Demonstrative Pronouns

When you are referring to something nonspecific ("*That's* not true!") or when you don't or can't know the name of the referent ("What is *this?*"), you will need to use the neuter demonstrative pronoun. In other words, because there is no direct referent, it cannot be stated and thus must be expressed as a neuter demonstrative pronoun.

The neuter demonstrative pronouns are:

esto (this)   **eso** (that)   **aquello** (that over there)

You will generally find demonstrative pronouns used in exclamations, questions and abstractions.

examples:

¡**Esto** es absurdo!   ¿Qué es **eso**?
This is absurd!   What is *that?*

Aquello es una monstruosidad.
That (unspecified thing far away) is a monstrosity.

No tengo dinero, por **eso** no puedo ir.
I don't have any money, *that* is why I can't go.

ejercicio   I-5-2

1. This is great! _____

2. What is this? _____

3. That is a crime (*el crimen*). _____

4. I never do that. _____

5. This is a sin (*el pecado*). _____

6. What is happening (*pasar*) with that (*thing far away*)? _____

7. That is why you (*s., fam.*) should vote. _____

8. This is why I shouldn't smoke. _____

9. Who says that? _____

10. Who wrote this? _____

traducción   I-5-3

"Who needs this? This is so stupid! I don't need this for my job." Some people say this when they are frustrated or when they have to take a class in the university that they don't want to take. It's this class or that (*one*). It's this professor or that (*one*). It's these books or those. It's these assignments or those. When does this end? Does this end after (*the*) graduation? Unfortunately, no. This is often an attitude for (*the*) life.

vocabulario

assignment	**la tarea**	job	**el trabajo**
attitude	**la actitud**	life	**la vida**
class	**la clase**	often	**a menudo**
(to) end	**terminar**	professor	**el/la profesor/a**
frustrated	**frustrado/a**	stupid	**estúpido**
graduation	**la graduación**	unfortunately	**desgraciadamente**

_____

_____

_____

_____

_____

_____

_____

_____

_____

_____

_____

_____

_____

_____

_____

_____

_____

_____

_____

_____

_____

Numbers as Pronouns

Numbers can function as pronouns when they stand for the number as well as a noun that either is understood or has been omitted. Both cardinal and ordinal numbers can serve this function.

Cardinal Numbers	Ordinal Numbers
uno/a	primero/a
dos	segundo/a
tres	tercero/a
cuatro	cuarto/a
cinco	quinto/a
seis	sexto/a
siete	séptimo/a
ocho	octavo/a
nueve	noveno/a
diez	décimo/a

Note: The cardinal numbers continue on to infinity. However, after the tenth, the ordinal numbers offer you two possibilities: either continue on—**onceavo, doceavo, treceavo,** etc.—or simply place the cardinal number alone or after the noun.

Quiero **el décimo.**　　Quiero **el once.**
I want *the tenth one.*　　I want *the eleventh one.*

Vivo en **el onceavo piso** (el piso once).
I live on *the eleventh floor.*

Cardinal Numbers as Pronouns

When used as pronouns, cardinal numbers include the significance of the understood noun, for example: How many children do you have? I have *three.* In this case, *three* represents "three children." Remember that when you use the number **uno** as a pronoun, it changes to **una** when replacing a feminine noun. All the other numbers do not.

¿Cuántos libros lees tú al año? Leo **uno.**
How many books do you read each year? I read *one.*

¿Estas galletas son para la fiesta? Pues, sólo comí **una.**
These cookies are for the party? Well, I only ate *one.*

ejercicio   I-6-1

Unless otherwise indicated, you = second-person singular.

1. A: How many cars do you have? B: I have one.

   _____

2. A: How many houses do you have? B: I have one.

   _____

3. A: How many cookies do you want? B: I want ten.

   _____

4. A: How many hamburgers do you (*pl., formal*) want? B: Jane wants two and I want one.

   _____

5. A: How many people are there in your family? B: There are three.

   _____

6. He has seven dogs, but I only have six.

   _____

7. He sees many stars (*la estrella*) in the sky (*el cielo*), but I see only one.

   _____

8. María knows (*conocer*) all these paintings (*la pintura*), but we know only one.

   _____

9. I only have one telephone, but one is better than nothing.

   _____

10. A: How many cards (*el naipe*) do you want? B: I want one.

   _____

Ordinal Numbers as Pronouns

When the ordinal number is an adjective, it precedes the noun, which is always in its singular form and agrees with it in gender: **el segundo libro; la segunda iglesia.** When this noun is omitted and the adjective becomes a pronoun, the meaning of the noun is understood, its gender is shown in the **-o** or **-a** ending, and the article is retained: **el segundo libro** becomes **el segundo.**

Tienes el primer* libro y el tercer* libro, y yo tengo **el segundo.**
You have the first book and the third book, and I have *the second.*

Ella vive en la cuarta casa y él vive en **la quinta.**
She lives in the fourth house, and he lives in *the fifth.*

———————

*As adjectives, the ordinals **primero** and **tercero** drop the -o when preceding a singular, masculine noun.

ejercicio   I-6-2

Based on the numbered order of the pictures, complete each sentence with the appropriate ordinal pronoun. The first one has been done for you.

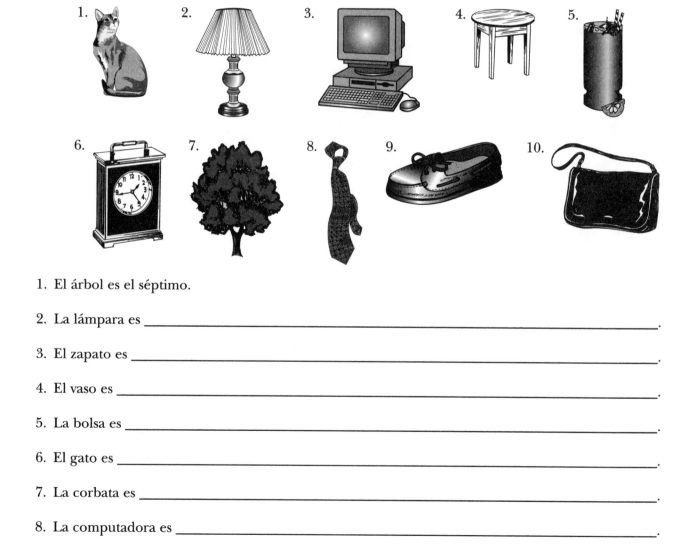

1. El árbol es el séptimo.

2. La lámpara es _____.

3. El zapato es _____.

4. El vaso es _____.

5. La bolsa es _____.

6. El gato es _____.

7. La corbata es _____.

8. La computadora es _____.

9. El reloj es _____.

10. La mesa es _____.

ejercicio   I-6-3

1. I live in the second house on the left (*a la izquierda*), and Miguel lives in the sixth.

   _____

2. A: Who lives in the eighth house? B: I don't know, but Marcos lives in the seventh.

   _____

3. My car is the third (*one*) on the right (*a la derecha*), and Ricardo's car is the fourth (*one*).

   _____

4. The Bible says that Adam (*Adán*) is the first person and that Eve (*Eva*) is the second.

   _____

5. The first movie (*la película*) is always better than (*mejor que*) the second.

   _____

6. The actor's third movie is better than the fourth.

   _____

7. His fifth book is more interesting than the sixth.

   _____

8. In Spain, the first day of the week is Monday, and the seventh is Sunday.

   _____

9. The eighth month is August, the ninth is September, and the tenth is October.

   _____

10. The first puzzle (*el enigma*) is harder (*más difícil*) than the second.

    _____

11. Today is the first (*day*) of April.

    _____

12. The first time (*la vez*) is always better than the second, the third, and so on (*y así sucesivamente*).

    _____

traducción   I-6-4

Whenever we eat together, my friend and I compete (*in order*) to see who can eat more. For example, when we eat crackers, if I eat one, he eats two. Then I eat three, and he eats four. The first contestant who finishes all the crackers is the winner. This is easy with crackers or grapes or cherries. But it is very difficult with hamburgers. The first is delicious. The second is, too. The third is not bad. The fourth is a challenge. The fifth is absurd, also the sixth, the seventh, and the eighth. The ninth is pure torture. And the tenth is impossible. It's worse with pies!

vocabulario

absurd	**absurdo/a**	hamburger	**la hamburguesa**
challenge	**el reto**	in order to	**para**
cherry	**la cereza**	pie	**el pastel**
compete	**competir**	pure	**puro/a**
contestant	**el/la participante**	raisin	**la pasa**
cracker	**la galleta**	together	**juntos/as**
delicious	**sabroso/a**	torture	**la tortura**
finish	**terminar**	winner	**el/la ganador/a**
for example	**por ejemplo**	worse	**peor**
grape	**la uva**		

_____

_____

_____

_____

_____

_____

_____

_____

_____

_____

Adjective Pronouns

FUNCTION: Assume the meaning of understood, irrelevant, or omitted nouns

SPANISH PLACEMENT: Preceding the verb as the subject or following the verb as the object of a sentence

ENGLISH EQUIVALENTS: the red one, somebody (See examples throughout.)

It is said that by nature human beings are efficient. That efficiency is found in virtually all uses of pronouns: a pronoun replaces an understood noun, which means that usually there is a trade. Using a pronoun for an understood noun lightens the load, so to speak.

I see Martin, Lisa, Carol, and Tina.
I see *them.*

The Qualitative Adjective Pronoun

In Spanish, this efficiency is perhaps seen best when descriptive, or qualitative, adjectives become pronouns. In English, we generally add the word *one,* as in "He has the green apple, and I have the red *one.*" In Spanish, the adjective assumes the entire meaning of the noun: **Él tiene la manzana verde y yo tengo *la roja*.** The adjective retains the gender and number of the omitted noun, as well as the appropriate definite article (**el, la, los,** or **las**).

examples:

Él lee el libro grande, y yo leo **el pequeño.**
He reads the big book, and I read *the small one.*

A mí me gusta la mesa azul, pero a ti te gusta **la roja.**
I like the blue table, but you like *the red one.*

Tú llevas zapatos negros y yo llevo **los blancos.**
You wear black shoes and I wear *white ones.*

Nosotros pintamos las casas enormes y ellos pintan **las muy pequeñas.**
We paint the enormous houses, and they paint *the very small ones.*

ejercicio   I-7-1

Unless otherwise indicated, you = second-person singular.

1. He buys new cars, but I always buy used ones.

   _____

2. She prefers tall men, but I prefer short ones.

   _____

3. They want the easy question, but we want the difficult one.

   _____

4. She thinks that the blond (*rubio*) man is handsome, but I prefer the brunette (*moreno*).

   _____

5. The blue fountain pen is yours, but the green one is mine.

   _____

6. Every client (*el cliente*) wants to buy a luxury (*de lujo*) car, but buys the compact one.

   _____

7. More people buy the gray carpet (*la alfombra*) because the white is always dirty (*sucio*).

   _____

8. The two dresses are beautiful, but the long (*largo*) one is more elegant.

   _____

9. He puts the big lamps (*la lámpara*) in the living room and the small ones in the bedroom.

   _____

10. The big glass (*la copa*) is for the red wine, and the small one is for the white (*wine*).

    _____

The Quantitative Adjective Pronoun

Adjectives that are quantitative tell us the number or amount of the noun to which they refer. When a number is in front of a noun (*two* cats), that number functions as an adjective. When the noun is understood and dropped, the adjective takes on the status of a pronoun because it includes the meaning of the noun. (See Unit 6 for more about numbers as pronouns.)

Yo tengo tres cajas y él tiene **cuatro.**
I have three boxes and he has *four* (boxes).

Hay dos mesas allí, pero sólo **una*** aquí.
There are two tables there, but only *one* (table) here.

---

*Note that the number **uno** (one) takes gender. This is the only number that does.

Many quantitative adjectives are not actual numbers themselves; rather, they refer to an amount or have a less direct manner of revealing number. Most of these words can function as adjectives: **algunos platos** (some plates), **todos los invitados** (all the guests). When they stand alone or are used to refer to a noun or other antecedent, they function as pronouns: **algunos** (some of them), **todos** (all of them). Listed below are many commonly used quantitative adjectives:

algunos/as	some (of them); any (of them)
ambos/as	both (of them)
cada uno/a	each one
demasiado/a	too much
demasiados/as	too many
los demás; las demás	the rest (of them)
los dos; las dos	both; the two (of them)
más	more (of it, of them)
la mayoría	the majority (of people)
menos	less; fewer
mucho/a	a lot (of something)
muchos/as	a lot (of things); many things
nada	nothing
ninguno/a	none; neither one; not anything; not a single one
otro/a	another; the other (one)
poco/a	(a) little
primero/a	first
todo/a	everything; all
último/a	last
unos/as	some
unos/as cuantos/as	a few (of them)
varios/as	several

examples:

A él le gusta el vestido rojo más que el verde, pero a mí me gustan **ambos.**
He likes the red dress more than the green one, but I like *both* (of them).

Jorge come todas las galletas en el paquete, pero Felipe come sólo **unas cuantas.**
Jorge eats all the cookies in the package, but Felipe eats only *a few* (of them).

Cada año intento ahorrar dinero, pero acabo por gastar **demasiado.**
Every year I try to save money, but I end up spending *too much* (of it).

Todos los miembros querían participar en el comité, pero **ninguno** quería trabajar duro.
All the members wanted to be on the committee, but *none* wanted to work hard.

ejercicio   **1-7-2**

1. Some people live in the city and some (*of them*) live in the country (*el campo*).

   _____

2. Seventy percent (*el...por ciento*) of the dentists use this toothbrush (*el cepillo de dientes*), and the rest (*of them*) use a stick (*el palo*).

   _____

3. I can't decide which is the better dishwasher (*el lavaplatos*). I like them both.

   _____

4. I never go shopping (*ir de compras*) with her. She buys everything. It's dangerous (*peligroso*).

   _____

5. Diego likes parties. He's always the last (*one*) to leave (*en salir*).

   _____

6. My husband drinks milk all the time. Therefore (*por eso*) I buy a lot (*of it*) every week.

   _____

7. I have several Spanish books. Do you want one?

   _____

8. Esmeralda loves (*encantar*) shoes. She has lots (*of them*).

   _____

9. In the meetings (*la reunión*), a few people talk all the time, and the majority (*of them*) suffer in silence.

   _____

10. Marcia receives all the presents and poor little (*pobrecita*) Jan doesn't receive a single one.

    _____

11. We have lots of salad. Do you want more (*of it*)?

    _____

12. Usually, thousands (*miles*) of people come to the ceremony, but this year there are obviously (*obviamente*) fewer.

    _____

13. The students are going on a field trip (*de excursión*). Each one has a backpack (*la mochila*).

_____

14. Each girl (*la chica*) has a pencil, but several (*of them*) don't have paper.

_____

15. I'm going to order (*pedir*) another milkshake (*el batido*). Do you want another (*one*), too?

_____

Adjective Pronouns that Refer to Unspecified People

When a pronoun replaces a known person, we often use a subject, or personal, pronoun. Instead of *John*, we use *he;* for *John and Carlos*, we use *they*, and so on.

Frequently, however, we speak of people whose names we do not know, cannot know, or whose identity, considering the situation, is irrelevant. When this is the case, you may use one of the following pronouns:

alguien	someone; somebody
cualquiera	anyone; anybody; any one (person)
cualesquiera	any (*pl.*)
el/la que	the one who; he/she who
los/las que	they who; those who; the ones who
el/la mayor	the oldest (one)
el/la menor	the youngest (one)
nadie	no one (person)
ninguno/a	neither one
todos/as	everyone; everybody

examples:

El mayor recibe todos los privilegios.
The oldest (one) receives all the privileges.

Santa Claus tiene regalos para **todos.**
Santa Claus has gifts for *everybody*.

El que cree esto, está loco.   **Nadie** va de compras aquí.
He who believes this, is crazy.   *No one* goes shopping here.

Cualquiera de mis amigos puede hablar español.
Any one of my friends can speak Spanish.

Cualesquiera de ustedes harían lo mismo.
Any of you would do the same thing.

ejercicio   I-7-3

1. Often (*a menudo*) the youngest (*m.*) wears used clothing.

   _____

2. Everybody thinks that this is brilliant.

   _____

3. Nobody is going to eat this. It's moldy (*mohoso*)!

   _____

4. Someone is in the kitchen with Dinah.

   _____

5. Our favorite customer (*la cliente*) is she who spends (*gastar*) all her money on cosmetics (*los cosméticos*) and clothing.

   _____

6. On *The Waltons,* John Boy is the oldest and Erin is the youngest.

   _____

7. For these positions (*el puesto*), those who want to work ten hours a day (*al día*) can request (*pedir*) an interview (*la entrevista*).

   _____

8. Many psychologists (*el psicólogo*) study the differences between the oldest (*child*) and the youngest (*child*) in the family.

   _____

9. Oscar Wilde writes that a cynic (*el cínico*) is he who knows the price (*el precio*) of everything and the value (*el valor*) of nothing.

   _____

10. Everyone suffers from time to time (*de vez en cuando*), and the majority are stronger for (*por*) the experience.

   _____

11. Everybody is here, but some (*of them*) don't know anybody.

   _____

12. Juan and Mateo live together, but neither (*one*) has a television set (*el televisor*).

_____

13. Anybody can wear these pants.

_____

14. Ramón gives advice (*dar consejos*) to anyone.

_____

15. There is a party tonight. Any (*pl.*) of you can go with me.

_____

Adjective Pronouns that Refer to Unspecified Things

When the name of the referent is either unknown or irrelevant, you will need a nonspecific, gender-neutral pronoun, such as the following:

algo	something; anything
cualquiera	anything; any thing; whichever; whatever
cualesquiera	any (*pl.*)
lo mejor	the best (thing)
lo mismo	the same (thing)
lo peor	the worst (thing)
nada	nothing; not anything

examples:

Puedes tener **cualquiera** de estas galletas.
You can have *any one* of these cookies.

Cuando vamos de vacaciones, siempre hacemos **lo mismo.**
When we go on vacation, we always do *the same thing*.

Lo mejor en la vida es gratis.
The best in life is free. (The best things in life are free.)

Tengo **algo** para ti.
I have *something* for you.

ejercicio   1-7-4

Unless otherwise indicated, you = second-person singular.

1. Do you have anything for (*para*) me? _____

2. Of all the things in the world, the best is love. _____

_____

3. It doesn't matter (*no importa*) if I wear bluejeans (*blue-jeans*). She always wears the same (*thing*).

_____

4. A: Which one do they want? B: Whatever. It doesn't matter. _____

_____

5. It's wonderful when you (*pl., formal*) dance. The best is when you dance the mambo. _____

_____

6. The service (*el servicio*) and the ambience (*el ambiente*) here are terrible. But the worst is the food.

_____

7. He never brings anything to a party, but he always eats and drinks everything. _____

_____

8. The worst (*thing*) in a relationship (*la relación*) is not to be able to trust (*tener confianza en*) the

   other person. _____

9. Some people think that he's very wise (*sabio*), but the truth is that he always says the same thing.

_____

10. I don't know anything about (*acerca de*) this. _____

11. Any one of these cars is good for (*para*) the winter. _____

_____

12. These books are interesting. You can read any one of them. _____

_____

13. Any one of these three is OK. _____

14. Any (*pl.*) of these are OK. _____

traducción   I-7-5

This sign says, "Today is the first day of the rest of your life." If this is true, then what is tomorrow? The second? I can't believe everything that I read. No one can. Some (*people*) believe everything. Some people believe the ads in the backs of magazines. I suppose that some of these are true, but the majority of these ads are lies. Who are these hucksters? They promise everything and deliver nothing.

vocabulario

ad	**el anuncio**	(to) promise	**prometer**
back	**la contraportada**	(the) rest of	**(el) resto de**
(to) deliver	**entregar**	sign	**el letrero**
huckster	**la persona no honrada**	(to) suppose	**suponer**
lie	**la mentira**	true	**la verdad**
life	**la vida**		

Relative Pronouns

The pronouns we will deal with in this unit all refer to something either previously stated or understood, and thus are related to that referent. For this reason, these pronouns are called relative pronouns.

que	that; who; which
el cual, la cual	the one who; the one which
los cuales, las cuales	those who; those which
el que, la que	the one who; the one which
los que, las que	those who; those which
lo que	that which; what; whatever
preposición + quien(es)	*preposition* + whom
preposición + que	*preposition* + that/which
cuyo, cuya, cuyos, cuyas	whose

Restrictive vs. Nonrestrictive Clauses

Before we proceed with any of these pronouns, it is necessary to understand the concepts of restrictive and nonrestrictive clauses. A grasp of these concepts will facilitate your work in this unit and allow you to make sense of its many parts.

Restrictive clause: A restrictive clause contains information that is essential to the meaning of the sentence. In other words, it restricts the meaning of the word(s) to which it refers. If this clause were removed, the sentence either would change meaning or become meaningless or ridiculous.

A lamp *that doesn't have a bulb* is useless.

In this sentence, the dependent clause "that doesn't have a bulb" is restrictive because it is necessary to the overall meaning of the sentence. If we remove this clause, we are left with the independent clause "A lamp is useless," which still is a grammatically correct sentence, but the essential meaning has changed dramatically, and what remains is absurd.

Nonrestrictive clause: A nonrestrictive clause contains information that is usually helpful to the overall meaning of the sentence; however, it is not essential. If a nonrestrictive clause were removed, the sentence would stand on its own.

Cats, *which sometimes live fifteen years or longer,* make nice pets.

The dependent clause, "which sometimes live fifteen years or longer," although informative, does not change the basic meaning of the independent clause (sentence), "Cats make nice pets." The dependent clause is not essential for us to understand the sentence; thus, it could be left out. Because the information contained in a nonrestrictive clause is not necessary to the overall meaning of the sentence, the nonrestrictive clause usually is set off from the main sentence by commas.

The Use of *que* in Clauses

The relative pronouns that separate clauses and mean "that," "who," and "which" in English all translate as **que** in Spanish. There is no distinction between living (who) and nonliving (that/which) referents as there is in English in this context.

examples:

el caballo **que** gana la carrera
the horse *that* wins the race

los estudiantes **que** leen el capítulo
the students *who* read the chapter

el lago, **que** está contaminado,
the lake, *which* is polluted,

The relative pronoun **que** sets up both restrictive and nonrestrictive clauses.

Note that in English the relative pronoun is sometimes omitted. Either one of the following is correct: "I have the towels you need" "I have the towels *that* you need." In Spanish, however, the relative pronoun cannot be omitted; you must include **que.**

examples:

Tengo las toallas **que** necesitas.
I have the towels you need.

Compramos la comida **que** pides.
We buy the food you request.

Él es el hombre **que** escribe esto.
He is the man *who* writes this.

Ellos venden casas **que** cuestan mucho.
They sell houses *that* cost a lot.

ejercicio   I-8-1

In this exercise, you = second-person singular.

1. I have the book that you want. _____

2. The people who work here are very nice (*amable*). _____

_____

3. The car that I want is red. _____

4. I only watch movies that are from Europe. _____

5. He believes that this sauce (*la salsa*) is very hot (*picante*). _____

_____

6. The medicine that I take every morning tastes like (*saber a*) gasoline. _____

_____

7. You have two books that are good and two that are bad. _____

_____

8. The painting (*la pintura*) that you see is by Francisco Goya. _____

_____

9. He doesn't know that I have his wallet (*la billetera*). _____

_____

10. Do you know that butter is pure fat (*pura grasa*)? _____

_____

11. The man who lives in this house is an actor. _____

12. She always rents (*alquilar*) the movies that I recommend (*recomendar*). _____

_____

13. She is the old woman (*la vieja*) who lives in a shoe. _____

_____

14. The cats that have many toes (*dedos*) live in Key West, Florida. _____

_____

15. The people who vote have a lot of power (*el poder*). _____

_____

The Use of *el cual* or *el que* in Clauses

When the relative pronouns *that, which, who,* or *whom* introduce a nonrestrictive clause (information not essential to the overall meaning of the sentence), you can use **el cual (la cual, los cuales, las cuales)** or **el que (la que, los que, las que)** instead of the simple **que.**

El cual and **el que** are interchangeable. They are used primarily in writing or in formal speech (while **que** is used more in conversation), which lends a more formal tone to sentences. Using these forms also adds greater emphasis to the nonrestrictive clauses they introduce.

examples:

Este sofá, **el cual (el que)** es disponible en veinte colores, es muy popular este año.
This sofa, *which* is available in twenty colors, is very popular this year.

Tu sobrina, **la cual (la que)** recibe buenas notas, quiere ser maestra.
Your niece, *the one who* gets good grades, wants to be a teacher.

Estos huevos, **los cuales (los que)** tienen casi un año, están muy sabrosos.
These eggs, *which* are almost a year old, are very tasty.

Estas langostas, **las cuales (las que)** son de Maryland, están muy frescas.
These lobsters, *which* are from Maryland, are very fresh.

ejercicio   I-8-2

1. His wife, who is lovely, speaks four languages (*el idioma*).

   _____

2. Their dog, which is a poodle (*el perro de lana*), barks (*ladrar*) all the time.

   _____

3. Our house, which is one hundred years old, is known (*conocido*) for the ghosts (*el fantasma*) that live in the attic (*el desván*).

   _____

4. My rings (*el anillo*), which are silver (*de plata*), are from Taxco, Mexico.

   _____

5. Our books, which are still (*todavía*) in boxes, are very valuable (*valioso*).

   _____

6. The landlord (*el casero*), who also lives in this building (*el edificio*), is a very strange (*extraño*) man.

   _____

7. My neighbor's (*el vecino*) children, who are noisier (*más ruidosos*) than an airport (*el aeropuerto*), are little angels (*el angelito*) in church.

   _____

8. The poet (*f.*), who is the mother of two daughters, writes every day (*todos los días*) at midnight.

   _____

9. The White House, which is popular with tourists, is the home (*el hogar*) of the President of the United States.

   _____

10. These wines, which are from France, are ninety years old.

   _____

11. The paragraph, which I have just (*acabar de*) read, makes no sense (*tener sentido*).

_____

12. This attitude (*la actitud*) of apathy (*la indiferencia*), which I cannot tolerate, is contagious (*contagioso*).

_____

The Use of a Preposition + *quien* or *que*

When the relative pronoun is the object of a preposition, you will use the appropriate preposition + **quien,** when the referent is a person, or the preposition + **que,** when the referent is inanimate. A clause formed by the preposition + **quien** or **que** is a restrictive clause (its information is essential to the meaning of the sentence).

Both Spanish and English have a rule which states that one should not end a sentence (or a question) with a preposition. Spanish distinguishes itself in that it honors this rule. We often are not so careful in English. In the examples below, the English, though not always technically proper, reflects contemporary usage; in other words, you will find a preposition at the end of the sentences. Note that in all cases the Spanish preposition is contained within the sentence.

examples:

Él es el hombre **con quien** trabajo.
He is the man I work *with.* / He is the man *with whom* I work.

Éste es el libro **en que** pienso.
This is the book that I'm thinking *about.* / This is the book *about which* I'm thinking.

Juana es la mujer **a quien** envío la comida.
Juana is the woman I'm sending the food *to.* / Juana is the woman *to whom* I'm sending the food.

Paco Ortiz es el hombre **por quien** voy a votar.
Paco Ortiz is the man I'm going to vote *for.* / Paco Ortiz is the man *for whom* I'm going to vote.

Antonio es el hombre **a* quien** amo.
Antonio is the man I love. / Antonio is the man *whom* I love.

Iris y Carmen son las chicas **a* quienes** conozco.
Iris and Carmen are the girls I know. / Iris and Carmen are the girls *whom* I know.

_____

*personal **a**

 **ejercio**   I-8-3

The Spanish syntax is given in parentheses. Note: You = second-person singular.

1. Kitty is the woman I live with. (Kitty is the woman with whom I live.)

_____

2. Who is the man you live with? (Who is the man with whom you live?)

_____

3. These are the people he works for (*para*). (These are the people for whom he works.)

_____

4. The man on the left is the person I date (*salir con*). (The man on the left is the person with whom I go out [date].)

_____

5. Margo is the woman I work for. (Margo is the woman for whom I work.)

_____

6. Francisco is the man I'm thinking about (*pensar en*). (Francisco is the man about whom I'm thinking.)

_____

7. Raúl is the boy (*el chico*) I'm angry with (*estar enojado/a con*). (Raúl is the boy with whom I'm angry.)

_____

8. Bárbara is the person I sympathize with (*tener compasión por*). (Bárbara is the person with whom I sympathize.)

_____

9. Ana is the woman I see.

_____

10. Those men are the players I watch.

_____

The Use of *lo que*

Lo que, which means "that which," "what," or "whatever," is a neuter relative pronoun that allows you to refer to a great abstraction, as in "You can have *whatever* you want"; or to encompass the entirety of something that is said or done, as in "*What* you are doing is a sin."

Note that when **lo que** is used to mean "whatever," it often stands for something that is unknown or doubtful and is followed by a verb in the subjunctive: **Haz *lo que puedas*** (Do *whatever you can*).

examples:

Lo que dices es interesante.
What you're saying is interesting.

¿Tienen **lo que** necesito?
Do you have *what* I need?

Él siempre hace **lo que** quiera.
He always does *whatever* he wants (may want).

Lo que quieres no existe.
What you want doesn't exist.

ejercicio   I-8-4

In each sentence, the word in bold type will translate as **lo que.** *(You = second-person singular.)*

1. He never remembers (*recordar*) **what** I want. _____

2. She always eats **what** I eat. _____

3. On your birthday, you can ask for (*pedir*) **whatever** you (may) want. _____

4. **Whatever** he says is always a lie (*la mentira*). _____

5. Do you hear **what** I hear? Do you know **what** I know? _____

6. He doesn't understand (*comprender*) **what** he reads. _____

7. Some people always do **what** they shouldn't do. _____

8. Do you know **what** you want to do this weekend? _____

9. She eats exactly **what** is bad for (*para*) her. _____

10. **What** you need is a hug (*el abrazo*). _____

The Use of *cuyo, cuya, cuyos, cuyas*

The relative pronoun **cuyo** (which means "whose") separates the owner and that which is owned: "Peter, whose thesis is brilliant, is a fascinating man." In this sentence, Peter is the owner, and the thesis is the object owned. The word *whose* begins the clause, and the form of **cuyo** must agree with the noun that immediately follows it.

The relative pronouns **cuyo, cuya, cuyos,** and **cuyas** nearly always introduce or set up a nonrestrictive clause.

examples:

Pedro, **cuya tesis** es brillante, es un hombre fascinante.
Pedro, *whose thesis* is brilliant, is a fascinating man.

Jean, **cuyo padre** es de París, habla francés.
Jean, *whose father* is from Paris, speaks French.

George, **cuyos abuelos** son músicos profesionales, toca bien el piano.
George, *whose grandparents* are professional musicians, plays the piano well.

Laura, **cuyas alfombras** tienen manchas, está muy enojada.
Laura, *whose rugs* have stains, is very angry.

ejercicio   I-8-5

Unless otherwise indicated, you = second-person singular.

1. Marcos, whose mother is a dentist, wants to sell candy (*los dulces*).

   _____

2. The boy (*el chico*), whose book you have, is my cousin.

   _____

3. The actor, whose movies are terrible, is very rich.

   _____

4. The dentist, whose office (*el consultorio*) is in the city, lives in the suburbs (*las afueras*).

   _____

5. The children, whose parents speak only English, study Spanish.

   _____

6. He is the man whose dog always steals (*robar*) our newspaper.

   _____

7. Are you (*s., formal*) the woman whose tree is so (*tan*) beautiful?

   _____

8. Are they the children whose father is the senator (*el senador*) from Colorado?

   _____

9. The student, whose teacher (*f.*) is from Ecuador, wants to go to Quito this summer.

   _____

10. Old Mrs. Hubbard, whose cupboards (*el gabinete*) are bare (*vacío*), wants to give her dog a bone (*el hueso*).

    _____

11. Mark, whose father is president of a bank, cannot add (*sumar*).

    _____

12. Lilia, whose store is very popular, is my best friend.

    _____

ejercicio   I-8-6

Fill in each blank with one of the following relative pronouns: **que, lo que, cuyo/a/os/as,** *preposition +* **quien.**

1. El libro _____ yo tengo es muy interesante.

2. Tú no tienes _____ necesitamos.

3. Las personas _____ viven en casas de cristal no deben tirar piedras.

4. Pedro, _____ coche está descompuesto, tiene que tomar el autobús.

5. Él es el hombre _____ yo estimo mucho.

6. Ellas son las compañeras _____ trabajo.

7. La mujer, _____ cara puedes ver en esta foto, es una espía internacional.

8. ¡_____ él dice es basura! ¡No sabe nada!

9. Casi todo el mundo cree _____ es necesario tener electricidad en la casa.

10. Mi canción favorita de Navidad se llama, "¿Oyes _____ yo oigo?"

11. En Noche Vieja (*New Year's Eve*), siempre hacemos _____ nos da la gana.

12. Hay muchas personas _____ hablan más de un idioma.

13. Mateo es el hombre _____ yo conozco bien.

14. Creo que tengo exactamente _____ ellos desean.

15. Este hombre, _____ corazón está roto, es un hombre trágico.

traducción   I-8-7

Cabo San Lucas, which is on the southern tip of Baja California, is a wonderful place for a tranquil vacation. The area, which is mostly desert, has many elegant resorts that have swimming pools, restaurants, bars, shops, and health clubs. For the most part (*En su mayor parte*), you (*s., formal*) can do whatever you want in the privacy of your hotel room. There is a downtown, which is somewhat small, that has a marina, which has many boats for fishing. Tourists who want to fish can rent a boat with a guide. Any person whose idea of fun is warmth and sun can be very content for a week in Cabo San Lucas.

vocabulario

any	**cualquier**	privacy	**la soledad**
area	**el área** (*f.*)	(to) rent	**alquilar**
bar	**el bar**	resort	**el resorte**
boat	**el barco**	shop	**la tienda**
desert	**el desierto**	somewhat	**algo**
downtown	**el centro**	southern	**sureño/a**
(to) fish	**ir de pesca**	swimming pool	**la piscina**
for fishing	**para la pesca**	tip	**la punta**
fun	**la diversión**	tranquil	**tranquilo/a**
guide	**el guía**	vacation	**las vacaciones**
health club	**el club**	warmth	**el calor**
place	**el lugar**		

Direct Object Pronouns

The direct object answers the question *What?* or *Whom?* with regard to the verb in a sentence or clause. Consider the sentence, "John has the book." *What* does John have? He has the book; thus, the book is the direct object. The direct object pronoun *it* can therefore replace the direct object noun in the sentence, "John has it."

In the sentence, "John sees Mary," one can ask, "*Whom* does John see?" John sees Mary; thus, Mary is the direct object. The direct object pronoun *her* can replace Mary in the sentence, "John sees her."

Singular	Plural
me (me) **te** (you) **lo/la** (him/her; you; it)	**nos** (us) **os** (you) **los/las** (them; you)

Placement in Affirmative Sentences

In an affirmative statement (or clause) with one verb, the direct object pronoun will immediately precede the conjugated verb.

examples:

Yo **te** conozco.
I know *you.*

Tú **me** amas.
You love *me.*

Ella **los** compra.
She buys *them.*

Lo vemos.
We see *him.*

La tenéis.
You have *it.*

Ustedes **lo** quieren.
You want *it.*

ejercicio   I-9-1

Fill in each blank with the appropriate direct object pronoun.

1. Juan tiene el libro.   Juan _____ tiene.

2. Ellos ven a María.   Ellos _____ ven.

3. Yo conozco a Jorge y a Felipe.   Yo _____ conozco.

4. Juanita conoce España.   Juanita _____ conoce.

5. Tú lavas la ropa.   Tú _____ lavas.

6. Tú compras los huevos.   Tú _____ compras.

7. Ustedes beben la leche.   Ustedes _____ beben.

8. Yo no veo los libros.   Yo no _____ veo.

9. Ellas tienen el dinero.   Ellas _____ tienen.

10. Vosotros comprendéis el ejercicio.   Vosotros _____ comprendéis.

11. Marta lleva el vestido a la fiesta.   Marta _____ lleva a la fiesta.

12. Yo uso la computadora cada día.   Yo _____ uso cada día.

13. Alejandro vende los zapatos.   Alejandro _____ vende.

14. Ella toma las vitaminas.   Ella _____ toma.

15. Nosotros miramos la televisión.   Nosotros _____ miramos.

ejercicio   I-9-2

1. I love you. _____

2. I love him. _____

3. He loves me. _____

4. I see you (*s., fam.*). _____

5. I know you (*s., formal*). _____

6. She sees him. _____

7. I drink it (*m.*). _____

8. I have it (*f.*). _____

9. You (*s., fam.*) have it (*m.*). _____

10. She has them (*m.*). _____

11. You love me. _____

12. I love her. _____

13. They love us. _____   17. They eat it (*f.*). _____

14. You (*s., fam.*) see me. _____   18. I want it (*m.*). _____

15. You (*pl., fam.*) know me. _____   19. We want it (*f.*). _____

16. We see her. _____   20. We have them (*f.*). _____

ejercicio   I-9-3

Answer the following questions using a direct object pronoun. Answer questions 4–15 in the affirmative.

1. ¿Dónde compras la ropa? _____

2. ¿Dónde compras los libros? _____

3. ¿Dónde estudias español? _____

4. ¿Conoces al Presidente de los Estados Unidos? _____

5. ¿Tomas un café cada día? _____

6. ¿Comprendes esta lección? _____

7. ¿Lees la revista *Teenbeat*? _____

8. ¿Lees el periódico cada día? _____

9. ¿Haces la cama cada día? _____

10. ¿Conoces la capital de España? _____

11. ¿Ves las estrellas ahora? _____

12. ¿Comes mucho pan? _____

13. ¿Miras las telenovelas (*soap operas*)? _____

14. ¿Lees poemas románticos a menudo? _____

Placement in Negative Sentences

In a negative sentence (or clause) with one verb, the direct object pronoun is placed between the word *no* (or other term of negation) and the conjugated verb.

examples:

Yo no lo sé.   **No lo** conocemos.
I do*n't* know *it*.   We do*n't* know *him*.

No los compras.
You do*n't* buy *them*.

Nunca lo estudiáis.
You *never* study *it*.

Él **no nos** ve **jamás.**
He *never* sees *us*.

Ellos **no me** odian.
They do*n't* hate *me*.

ejercicio   I-9-4

Unless otherwise indicated, you = second-person singular.

1. I don't have it (*m.*). _____

2. She doesn't see it (*f.*). _____

3. I don't know him. _____

4. You don't know me. _____

5. They don't buy it (*f.*). _____

6. He doesn't write it (*m.*). _____

7. They don't read them (*m.*). _____

8. She doesn't earn it (*m.*). _____

9. I don't wear it (*m.*). _____

10. We don't see you. _____

11. You don't have it (*f.*). _____

12. They don't see it (*m.*). _____

13. He doesn't know me. _____

14. They don't know us. _____

15. We don't use it (*m.*). _____

16. She doesn't read it (*m.*). _____

17. We don't sing them (*f.*). _____

18. You (*pl., formal*) don't have it (*m.*). _____

19. You never wear them (*m.*). _____

20. You never see us. _____

Placement in Affirmative Sentences with Two Verbs

In a statement (or clause) that contains two verbs—the first verb is conjugated and the second one remains in the infinitive form—you have two options:

1. Place the direct object pronoun immediately before the first verb (conjugated).

2. Attach the direct object pronoun directly to the second verb (infinitive).

Note: Both options are used in writing and in conversation; however, the second option is used more frequently.

examples:

Te quiero **ver.** / Quiero **verte.**
I want *to see you.*

Lo puedes **beber.** / Puedes **beberlo.**
You can *drink it.*

Él **nos** debe **visitar.** / Él debe **visitarnos.**
He should *visit us.*

Lo queremos **comprar.** / Queremos **comprarlo.**
We want *to buy it.*

La podéis **comer.** / Podéis **comerla.**
You can *eat it.*

Ellos **lo** deben **ver.** / Ellos deben **verlo.**
They should *see it.*

ejercicio   I-9-5

Fill in the blank with the direct object pronoun attached to the infinitive.

1. Yo necesito lavar la ropa. Yo necesito _____.

2. Tú quieres comer la pizza. Tú quieres _____.

3. Ella tiene que escribir el informe. Ella tiene que _____.

4. Debemos limpiar la casa. Debemos _____.

5. El pianista puede tocar las canciones. El pianista puede _____.

6. Ellos pueden bailar el tango. Ellos pueden _____.

7. Quiero construir los edificios aquí. Quiero _____ aquí.

8. El gato puede ver el ratón (*mouse*). El gato puede _____.

9. Ella quiere conocer a tu madre. Ella quiere _____.

10. Prefiero oír la verdad. Prefiero _____.

11. El profesor quiere ver a tu padre ahora. El profesor quiere _____ ahora.

12. La cocinera va a preparar las tortillas. La cocinera va a _____.

13. Nadie puede oír la música ahora. Nadie puede _____ ahora.

14. Ellos quieren conocer a mis hermanos. Ellos quieren _____.

15. Queremos visitar el museo. Queremos _____.

ejercicio   I-9-6

For items 1–5, place the direct object pronoun before the conjugated verb. For items 6–10, attach the direct object pronoun to the infinitive.

1. He wants to see me. _____

2. She wants to kiss him. _____

3. You (*s., fam.*) should eat them (*m.*). _____

4. They have to do it (*f.*). _____

5. We want to meet them (*f.*). _____

6. She has to sing it (*f.*). _____

7. I should read it (*m.*). _____

8. I want to see you (*s., fam.*) tomorrow. _____

9. They need to have it (*m.*) by (*para*) tomorrow. _____

10. Juan can see us. _____

Placement in Questions and Negative Sentences with Two Verbs

For questions and/or negative statements with two verbs, the direct object pronoun can be placed before the conjugated verb or attached directly to the infinitive.

examples:

No tengo que **leerlo.** / **No lo** tengo que leer.
I do*n't* have *to read it.*

No queremos **hacerlo.** / **No lo** queremos hacer.
We do*n't* want *to do it.*

¿Tienes que **estudiarlo** conmigo? / ¿**Lo** tienes que **estudiar** conmigo?
Do you have *to study it* with me?

¿Podéis **soportarlo?** / ¿**Lo** podéis **soportar?**
Can you *stand it?*

Usted **no** debe **ponerlo** aquí.   ¿Piensan en **venderlo?**
You should*n't put it* here.   Are you thinking of *selling it?*

ejercicio   I-9-7

For this exercise, attach the direct object pronoun to the infinitive form. Unless otherwise indicated, you = second-person singular.

1. Do you want to see it (*f.*) with me? _____

2. Are you going to eat it (*m.*)? _____

3. Should we drink it (*f.*) now, or should we put it in the refrigerator? _____

_____

4. Can we eat it (*m.*), or should we throw it into (*a*) the garbage? _____

_____

5. You shouldn't put them (*m.*) in the living room. _____

6. If you don't want to have it (*f.*), you should put it in the box and return (*devolver*) it. _____

_____

7. I can't wear them (*m.*) to a formal party. _____

8. Why can't you see me? _____

9. You don't have to do it (*m.*) today. _____

10. Do you want to open them (*f.*) in the morning and close them in the evening? _____

_____

ejercicio   I-9-8

For this exercise, place the direct object pronoun before the conjugated verb. Unless otherwise indicated, you = second-person singular.

1. I don't want to see you (*m., pl., formal*) tonight. _____

2. You shouldn't return (*devolver*) it (*f.*). _____

3. Why can't you say it (*m.*)? _____

4. We are not going to see her at (*en*) the library. _____

5. She can't throw them (*f.*) in (*a*) the garbage. _____

6. When can I see them (*f.*)? _____

7. If you don't want to hear it (*m.*), you can turn off (*apagar*) the radio. _____

_____

8. Where do you want to store (*guardar*) them (*m.*)? Can we put them here? _____

_____

9. Are you (*pl., formal*) going to sell it (*f.*)? _____

10. No, you cannot hit (*golpear*) him! _____

ejercicio   I-9-9

I know that Marcos has my money, my shoes, and the table and chairs for my dining room. He thinks (*believes*) that I don't know this, but, yes, I know it. First, the money. I know that he has it because I can see it in that drawer (*over there*). Second, the shoes. I need them because if I don't wear them, I can't run fast or (*ni*) jump well. Third, the table. I don't know why (*por qué*) he has it or (*ni*) why he wants it. I want to put it in my new house. He believes that the chairs are his, but it's not true. They are mine. And I want them now.

vocabulario

dining room	**el comedor**	now	**ahora**
drawer	**la gaveta**	second	**segundo**
first	**primero**	third	**tercero**
(to) jump	**saltar**	true	**verdad**

Indirect Object Pronouns

The indirect object answers the question *To* or *for whom?* or *To* or *for what?* with regard to the verb in a sentence or clause. Another way of looking at it is to say that the indirect object tells us where the direct object is going.

Consider the sentence, "I give you the gift (I give the gift *to* you)." The direct object is the gift, because this answers the question *What* (do I give)? The indirect object, then, is *you* because I am giving it (the gift) to you. *You* is where the gift is going.

In the sentence "He buys me flowers (He buys flowers *for* me)," the direct object is flowers (because that is what he buys), and the indirect object is me because I am the one *for whom* he buys the flowers.

The indirect object pronouns in Spanish are as follows:

Singular	Plural
me (me)	**nos** (us)
te (you)	**os** (you)
le (him; her; you; it)	**les** (them; you)

In a sentence with an indirect object, there is always a direct object, either stated or implied. In the sentence "My grandmother writes me every week," *me* is the indirect object because my grandmother is writing *something* (a note, a letter, a postcard, an e-mail message) *to me*. The direct object is understood.

ejercicio   I-10-1

In the following sentences, identify the direct object and the indirect object. Note that some direct objects are understood; please identify them.

	Direct Object	**Indirect Object**
1. John tells me a story.	_____	_____
2. She buys him nothing.	_____	_____
3. They send us food.	_____	_____
4. The chef cooks us a meal.	_____	_____
5. The cannibal cooks us for his friends.	_____	_____
6. He tells you.	_____	_____
7. I bought you a ring.	_____	_____
8. He buys drinks for everyone.	_____	_____
9. You write me every week.	_____	_____
10. They sold the diamonds to her.	_____	_____

Placement in Affirmative Sentences

In an affirmative statement (or clause) with one verb, the indirect object pronoun will immediately precede the conjugated verb.

Note that each of the following examples has two possible English translations. English allows for two ways to express the indirect object: (a) between the verb and the direct object and (b) in a prepositional phrase following the direct object.

examples:

Juan **me** compra un libro.
John buys *me* a book.
John buys a book *for me.*

Yo **te** digo la verdad siempre.
I always tell *you* the truth.
I always tell the truth *to you.*

Ella **le** escribe una carta.
She writes *him* a letter.
She writes a letter *to him.*

Ella **nos** dijo una mentira.
She told *us* a lie.
She told a lie *to us.*

Os damos el dinero.
We give *you* the money.
We give the money *to you.*

Él **les** canta una canción.
He sings *them* a song.
He sings a song *to them.*

ejercicio   I-10-2

Fill in each blank with the appropriate indirect object pronoun.

1. Jorge compra flores para mí. Jorge _____ compra flores.

2. Marta cuenta la historia a nosotros. Marta _____ cuenta la historia.

3. Los padres leen el libro al niño. Los padres _____ leen el libro.

4. Escribo una carta a mis abuelos. _____ escribo una carta.

5. Felipe da un anillo a Juana. Felipe _____ da un anillo.

6. Vendemos la casa a Marta. _____ vendemos la casa.

7. Traigo el maquillaje (*makeup*) a Mary Kay. _____ traigo el maquillaje.

8. Preparamos la cena para Guillermo. _____ preparamos la cena.

9. Compras la falda para mí. _____ compras la falda.

10. Martín planta un árbol para nosotros. Martín _____ planta un árbol.

11. Ella escribe una carta a ustedes. Ella _____ escribe una carta.

12. Enviamos el regalo a vosotros. _____ enviamos el regalo.

13. Sirvo la comida a ellas. _____ sirvo la comida.

14. El arquitecto diseña una casa para ti. El arquitecto _____ diseña una casa.

15. El mesero sirve la bebida a Isabel. El mesero _____ sirve la bebida.

ejercicio   I-10-3

1. I tell him the truth. _____

2. He tells lies to me all the time. _____

3. We give her the flowers. _____

4. I write them a letter every week. _____

5. They write to us every month. _____

6. She sings him a song. _____

7. John is my assistant (*el ayudante*), and I dictate (*dictar*) a letter to him. _____

_____

8. I always tell her that she's pretty. _____

9. I send them a card (*la tarjeta*) for their anniversary. _____

10. What do they give you (*s., fam.*) for your birthday every year? _____

_____

Placement in Negative Sentences

In a negative statement (or clause) with one verb, the indirect object pronoun is placed between the word *no* (or other term of negation) and the conjugated verb.

examples:

Él **no me** trae nada.
He doesn*'t* bring *me* anything.

La médica **no te** da medicina.
The doctor doesn*'t* give *you* medicine.

No le envío la cuenta **jamás.**
I *never* send *him* the bill.

Ellos **no nos** dicen la verdad.
They do*n't* tell *us* the truth.

Nunca os damos regalos.
We *never* give *you* gifts.

No les vendes el pan.
You do*n't* sell *them* the bread.

ejercicio   I-10-4

Unless otherwise indicated, you = second-person singular.

1. He doesn't tell me anything. _____

2. I don't tell him anything. _____

3. They never send him anything because they don't know his address. _____

_____

4. I don't give her money. _____

5. The waiter doesn't sing "Happy Birthday" to you. _____

_____

6. Why don't they tell her the truth? _____

7. Why don't they buy you (*pl., fam.*) a computer (*la computadora*)? _____

_____

8. I serve them dinner, but they never thank (*dar las gracias*) me. _____

_____

9. If you (*pl., formal*) don't ask me questions (*hacer preguntas*), I don't tell you lies. _____

_____

10. We don't lend (*prestar*) them money. _____

Placement in Affirmative Sentences with Two Verbs

In a statement (or clause) that contains two verbs—the first verb is conjugated and the second one remains in its infinitive form—you have two options:

1. Place the indirect object pronoun immediately before the first verb (conjugated).

2. Attach the indirect object pronoun directly to the second verb (infinitive).

Note: Both options are used in writing and in conversation; however, the second option is used more frequently.

examples:

Él quiere **darme** un regalo. / Él **me** quiere **dar** un regalo.
He wants *to give me* a gift.

Tú necesitas **comprarnos** algo. / Tú **nos** necesitas **comprar** algo.
You need *to buy us* something.

Puedo **decirte** todo. / **Te** puedo **decir** todo.
I can *tell you* everything.

Preferimos **prestaros** el dinero. / **Os** preferimos **prestar** el dinero.
We prefer *to lend you* the money.

Él quiere **venderle** el coche. / Él **le** quiere **vender** el coche.
He wants *to sell her* the car.

Ella debe **alquilarles** la casa. / Ella **les** debe **alquilar** la casa.
She should *rent* the house *to them*.

ejercicio   I-10-5

Fill in the blank with the indirect object pronoun attached to the infinitive.

1. Quiero dar el libro a Jorge. Quiero _____ el libro.

2. Necesitamos decir la verdad a ellos. Necesitamos _____ la verdad.

3. Ella tiene que prestar el dinero a mí. Ella tiene que _____ el dinero.

4. Debéis alquilar el barco a ellos. Debéis _____ el barco.

5. Nadie puede decir nada a ti. Nadie puede _____ nada.

6. Prefiero escribir una carta a Marta. Prefiero _____ una carta.

7. Ellos esperan cantar la canción a vosotros. Ellos esperan _____ la canción.

8. El presidente debe decir la verdad a nosotros. El presidente debe _____ la verdad.

9. La madre necesita mostrar el amor a su niño. La madre necesita _____ el amor.

10. Un cómico puede contar chistes (*jokes*) a nosotros. Un cómico puede _____ chistes.

11. El arquitecto va a diseñar una casa para mí. El arquitecto va a _____ una casa.

12. Voy a preparar paella para ustedes. Voy a _____ paella.

13. Voy a decir mi nombre a ellos. Voy a _____ mi nombre.

14. Juan sólo puede vender los cigarrillos a los adultos. Juan sólo puede _____ los cigarrillos.

15. El mesero debe servir la cena a nosotros con más rapidez. El mesero debe _____ la cena con más rapidez.

ejercicio   I-10-6

For items 1–5, place the indirect object pronoun before the conjugated verb. For items 6–10, attach the indirect object pronoun to the infinitive.

1. I want to give him a gift. _____

2. He needs to tell me the truth. _____

3. We should write her a letter. _____

4. You (*s., fam.*) should write to us more often (*más a menudo*). _____

_____

5. You (*pl., formal*) have to tell them the truth. _____

6. We should give them olive oil (*el aceite de oliva*). _____

7. He wants to buy her a diamond (*el diamante*). _____

8. When he comes to our house, he always wants to bring (*traer*) us something. _____

_____

9. I can send you (*s., fam.*) these vases (*el florero*) through the mail (*por correo*). _____

_____

10. You (*pl., fam.*) need to tell him something. _____

Placement in Questions and Negative Sentences with Two Verbs

For questions and/or negative statements with two verbs, the indirect object pronoun can be placed before the conjugated verb or attached directly to the infinitive.

examples:

¿Quién va a **enviarme** una cuenta? / ¿Quién **me** va a **enviar** una cuenta?
Who is going *to send me* a bill?

Él **no** necesita **darnos** la información. / Él **no nos** necesita **dar** la información.
He does*n't* need *to give us* the information.

¿Debemos **decirte** la verdad? / ¿**Te** debemos **decir** la verdad?
Should we *tell you* the truth?

No quiero **venderos** estos collares. / **No os** quiero **vender** estos collares.
I do*n't* want *to sell you* these necklaces.

Nunca podéis **comprarle** la felicidad. / **Nunca le** podéis **comprar** la felicidad.
You can *never buy* happiness *for her.*

No tengo que **decirles** nada. / **No les** tengo que **decir** nada.
I do*n't* have *to tell them* anything.

ejercicio   I-10-7

Use both options to express each statement or question. Unless otherwise indicated, you = second-person singular.

1. Do you want to bring me a kitten? _____

_____

2. We're not going to show them our new house. _____

_____

3. Do you want to sell them these paintings? _____

_____

4. Who is going to pay me the money? _____

_____

5. Can you send the furniture (*los muebles*) to us by (*para*) Tuesday? _____

_____

6. The artist can't paint her a picture (*el cuadro*) by June. _____

_____

7. I'm not going to wash your clothing for you. _____

_____

8. We don't want to tell you (*pl., formal*) the bad news (*las malas noticias*). _____

_____

9. When can you (*pl., fam.*) build (*construir*) the building (*el edificio*) for us? _____

_____

10. Should you read her such a letter (*tal carta*)? _____

_____

The Redundant Use of the Indirect Object Pronoun

Even though the principal purpose of any pronoun is to replace a noun, there are times when it is clearer or more emphatic to use both the noun or pronoun and **a** + the pronoun or noun. This is done primarily with the indirect object pronoun and more frequently with some verbs (see the following list). At such times, the indirect object is usually in the third person.

The following verbs frequently take both a noun or pronoun and **a** + the appropriate pronoun:

comprar	to buy	**mandar**	to send
dar	to give	**pedir**	to ask (a favor); to request (from)
decir	to say; to tell	**preguntar**	to ask (a question)
escribir	to write	**preparar**	to prepare
enviar	to send	**regalar**	to give (a gift)
hacer	to make or do	**traer**	to bring

examples:

Yo **le** doy **a Juan** cinco dólares.
I give *him* (*John*) five dollars.

Les pregunto **a ellos** si quieren ir.
I ask *them* if they want to go.

Manuel **les** escribe **a sus padres** cada semana.
Manuel writes to *them* (*his parents*) every week.

Le pido **a mi jefe** un aumento.
I ask *my boss* for a raise.

As you can see in the preceding examples, the addition of **a** + a noun or pronoun neither replaces nor adds necessary information. Thus, technically, it is redundant.

Since the redundant prepositional phrase is not necessary, why do we add it? One reason is that the third-person noun or pronoun helps us clarify the ambiguous, pronoun **le**. Another reason is that the prepositional phrase adds emphasis to the noun or pronoun. In other words, they help each other.

For clarity:

Le conté el chiste.	I told (*him? her? you?*) the joke.
Le conté **a Juan** el chiste.	I told *Juan* the joke.
Le conté el chiste **a él.**	I told *him* the joke.
Le conté el chiste **a usted.**	I told *you* the joke.
Le conté el chiste **a ella.**	I told *her* the joke.

For emphasis:

Juan **me** contó **a mí** ese chiste.	Juan told *me* that joke.
¿Juan **te** contó ese chiste **a ti?**	Juan told *you* that joke?
Juan **nos** contó ese chiste **a nosotros.**	Juan told *us* that joke.
Juan **les** contó ese chiste **a ellas.**	Juan told *them* that joke.

A final reason for using the redundant construction is that this is the way it's done. Perhaps this is not a satisfying answer in the rational sense; however, all languages, like all people, have their distinct charms that defy reason. The redundant use of **a** + a noun or pronoun is part of the charm of Spanish.

---

ejercicio   I-10-8

In a sentence with two verbs, choose one of the options (pronoun before the conjugated verb or attached to the infinitive) to express the sentence in Spanish. Unless otherwise indicated, you = second-person singular.

1. I tell Juan everything. _____

2. I want to tell him everything. _____

3. She writes to her aunt every month. _____

4. Why do you bring so much (*tanto*) to Mateo? _____

5. She gives the documents to her attorney (*el abogado*). _____

   _____

6. She has to give the money to the police (*la policía*). _____

7. Margarita is giving (*regalar*) us a TV set! _____

8. Oliver wants to give (*regalar*) me a watch from Cartier! _____

   _____

9. A: What are you making for (*a*) your friends? B: I'm making them a cake (*la torta*). _____

   _____

10. I bring them a newspaper every morning. _____

11. I usually buy them (*f.*) clothing for (*para*) Christmas. _____

_____

12. What should we buy her? _____

13. Romeo sends Julieta roses on Valentine's Day. _____

14. Are they going to send you (*pl., formal*) anything this year? _____

_____

15. George Washington cannot tell a lie (*la mentira*) to anyone. _____

_____

Indirect Object Pronouns with *gustar*

There is a group of Spanish verbs which, to the native English speaker's notion of syntax, work in reverse. The most commonly used of these verbs is **gustar** (to be pleasing to), hence the title of this section.

While in English, one says "I like the bread," in Spanish, to get this same message across, one says, **"Me gusta el pan,"** which literally means, "The bread is pleasing to me." The *bread* is now the subject, and *I* has become the indirect object.

Because the bread is pleasing to me—remember that the indirect object often contains or implies the preposition *to*—we will need the indirect object pronoun in this sentence, as well as in all sentences that use the verb **gustar** (and the other verbs that operate in the manner of **gustar**).

The key to the verbs in this section is to remember that they nearly always operate in the third-person singular and plural forms. The things being discussed have their effect on people: Chicago fascinates *me;* traffic bothers *you;* autobiographies interest *her;* money is not important *to him.*

To work with **gustar,** and verbs like it, you will use the following recipe:

indirect object pronoun + third-person (*s.* or *pl.*) verb + noun(s)

examples:

Singular Subject (noun)	**Plural Subject (noun)**	
Me **gusta la pintura.**	Me **gustan las pinturas.**	I like the painting(s).
Te **gusta el anillo.**	Te **gustan los anillos.**	You like the ring(s).
Le **gusta el zorro.**	Le **gustan los zorros.**	He/She likes the fox(es).
Nos **gusta la culebra.**	Nos **gustan las culebras.**	We like the snake(s).
Os **gusta la lámpara.**	Os **gustan las lámparas.**	You like the lamp(s).
Les **gusta el reloj.**	Les **gustan los relojes.**	They like the clock(s).

Notes:

1. In discussing actions that one likes to do, substitute an infinitive for the noun.

Me gusta **correr.**	No me gusta ni **correr** ni **nadar.**
I like *to run*.	I don't like *to run* or *swim*.

2. For clarification in the third person, precede the phrase with the preposition **a** + the person's name or the corresponding pronoun.

   A Madonna le gusta cantar.
   Madonna likes to sing.

   A Tom Hanks le gusta actuar. **A él** le gusta dirigir también.
   Tom Hanks likes to act. *He* also likes to direct.

3. Otherwise, adding the person's name or pronoun adds emphasis.

A mí me gusta el té.	**A ti** te gustan los deportes.
I (*emphasized*) like tea.	You (*emphasized*) like sports.

4. When what one likes is simply *it* (as in, "I like it"), *it* will not translate because technically the word *it* is the subject of the sentence ("It pleases me"), and *it* (or its plural form *they*) is understood.

Me gusta.	**Me gustan.**
I like it.	*I like them.*

¿Qué piensas tú? ¿Verdadero o falso?

_____ 1. Me gusta la comida mexicana.

_____ 2. Me gustan los dibujos animados (*cartoons*) en la televisión los sábados por la mañana.

_____ 3. No me gusta cuando una persona me llama por teléfono a las tres de la mañana.

_____ 4. Al Presidente de los Estados Unidos le gusta la política.

_____ 5. A Sherlock Holmes le gustan las intrigas.

_____ 6. En este país, normalmente nos gusta la democracia.

_____ 7. A muchas personas les gusta celebrar la Noche Vieja (*New Year's Eve*) en una fiesta.

_____ 8. A mí no me gusta ir de compras en una tienda muy grande.

_____ 9. A mi mejor amigo/a le gusta bailar en las discotecas.

_____10. A un abogado le gusta ganar los casos.

_____11. No me gusta ni bailar ni cantar delante de muchas personas.

_____12. A Donald Trump le gusta muchísimo el dinero.

ejercicio   I-10-9

*Use **gustar** to answer the following questions either affirmatively or negatively—whichever is true for you. Follow the pattern given in item 1 below.*

1. ¿Te gusta la leche? *Sí, me gusta la leche. / No, no me gusta la leche.* _____

_____

2. ¿Te gustan los dramas de Shakespeare? _____

3. ¿Te gusta comer en el coche? _____

4. ¿Te gusta limpiar la casa? _____

5. ¿Te gustan los platos (*dishes*) exóticos? _____

6. ¿Te gustan las películas de horror? _____

7. ¿Te gusta correr? _____

8. ¿Te gusta memorizar los verbos españoles? _____

9. ¿Te gustan los mosquitos? _____

10. ¿Te gusta conducir en la hora punta (*rush hour*)? _____

Other Verbs That Take the Indirect Object Pronoun

There are several Spanish verbs that operate in the manner of **gustar**—that is, they take the indirect object pronoun and demonstrate the effect that something or someone has on a person.

The most common of these verbs include the following:

bastar	to be sufficient/enough to; to suffice
caer bien (mal)	to like (dislike); to go well (badly) with
disgustar	to be disgusting to; to "hate" (a thing)
doler (o→ue)	to be painful to; to hurt
encantar	to be enchanting to; to "love" (a thing)
faltar	to be lacking to; to be missing to; to need (a thing)
fascinar	to be fascinating to
importar	to be important to
interesar	to be interesting to
molestar	to be bothersome to; to bother
parecer	to seem; to appear to
sobrar	to be left over to; to be in surplus
volver (o→ue) loco/a	to be crazy about or for (more intense than *encantar*)

¿Verdadero o falso?

_____ 1. Cuando me duele la cabeza, tomo una aspirina.

_____ 2. Me importa la verdad.

_____ 3. La arquitectura de Frank Lloyd Wright me fascina.

_____ 4. Los anuncios (*commercials*) en la televisión me molestan mucho.

_____ 5. Me disgustan las personas que gruñen (*grumble*) todo el tiempo.

_____ 6. A un millonario le sobra el dinero.

_____ 7. A los actores de Hollywood les encanta ganar el "Oscar".

_____ 8. Me falta el dinero para comprar un diamante de cinco quilates.

_____ 9. A muchos jugadores de tenis les duelen los codos.

_____10. No me importa tener mucho dinero ni vivir en una casa lujosa.

_____11. No me interesan los chismes (*gossip*).

_____12. A mí me parece que las joyas de Tiffany's son las mejores.

_____13. Me vuelve loco/a el chocolate.

_____14. A un elefante le bastan dos cacahuates (*peanuts*).

_____15. Me caen bien mis amigos.

_____16. Me cae mal la carne con chocolate.

ejercicio I-10-10

This exercise uses the verbs in the preceding list. Sometimes, clues to the appropriate verb are given in parentheses. Unless otherwise indicated, you = second-person singular.

1. This book fascinates me. _____

2. I don't want anything more. I have enough food. (*The food is sufficient for me.*) _____

_____

3. Mikey likes everything. _____

4. I hate this movie. (*This movie is disgusting to me.*) _____

_____

5. My eyes hurt. _____

6. Nothing is important to him and nothing interests him. How (*qué*) sad! _____

_____

7. I'm missing a button (*el botón*) on my shirt. _____

_____

8. We love your new house! _____

9. What's bothering you? _____

10. These magazines seem absurd (*absurdo*) to me. _____

_____

11. After the holidays (*los días de fiesta*), they don't have (*any*) money left over. _____

_____

12. He hates coffee, but I love it. _____

13. I'm crazy about this play (*la obra de teatro*). _____

_____

14. I don't like cookies with raisins. (*Cookies with raisins don't go well with me.*) _____

_____

15. She loves sports, but he hates them. _____

traducción   I-10-11

Note: The focus here is on indirect object pronouns; however, because these translations are cumulative, there will be direct object pronouns, as well as other types previously covered.

I have a new neighbor. He lives next door to me. He seems (*to me*) very nice. I want to give him something that he likes. I can make a cake for him or I can write him a note that says (*to him*), "Welcome to the neighborhood!" I can see him now. These binoculars are great! I can see it all now. I think that I'm going to watch him for a while. No one sees me when I use my binoculars because I turn out all the lights. I love these binoculars. I don't know what I ought to do. I'm going to ask my aunt what she thinks. She always gives me good advice.

vocabulario

(good) advice	**(buenos) consejos**	lights	**las luces**
(to) ask	**preguntar**	neighbor	**el vecino**
binoculars	**los prismáticos**	neighborhood	**el vecindario**
cake	**la torta**	next door to	**al lado de**
for a while	**por un rato**	note	**la nota**
(to) give (a gift)	**regalar**	(to) seem	**parecer**
great	**fantástico**	(to) turn out	**apagar**

Reflexive Object Pronouns

FUNCTION: Indicate that the subject (performer) and the object (receiver) of an action are the same person (or thing)

SPANISH PLACEMENT: Immediately before the conjugated verb or attached directly to the infinitive

English Equivalents: myself, yourself, himself, herself, itself, ourselves, themselves

Reflexive pronouns are tiny words that carry the power to change the meaning of a sentence.

Singular	Plural
me (myself) **te** (yourself) **se** (himself; herself; yourself)	**nos** (ourselves) **os** (yourselves) **se** (themselves; yourselves)

The principal function of the reflexive object pronoun is to indicate that the action being performed isn't going anywhere. If Jane washes your hair, her action has extended to you; thus, the action is not reflexive. However, when Jane washes her own hair, the action, which was begun by Jane, stays with Jane. Thus, in this case, the verb **lavarse,** which means "to wash," is reflexive and it requires a reflexive object pronoun.

Jane **te** lava el pelo.   Jane **se** lava el pelo.
Jane washes *your* hair.   Jane washes *her* hair.
(literally, Jane washes the   (literally, Jane washes the
hair on you.)   hair on herself.)

Reflexive Verbs in the Powder Room

Many of the standard reflexive verbs refer to the things we do routinely every day to prepare ourselves. The following are among the most common reflexive verbs in this category:

afeitarse	to shave oneself	**lavarse**	to wash oneself
bañarse	to bathe oneself	**peinarse**	to comb oneself (one's hair)
cepillarse	to brush oneself	**pesarse**	to weigh oneself
ducharse	to take a shower	**secarse**	to dry oneself

Note that when mentioning a body part, you use the definite article (**el, la, los, las**) instead of the possessive adjective (**mi, tu, su,** etc.). The reasons for this are twofold: first, if you are washing the hair on you, it has to be *your* hair, so it is redundant to use the possessive adjective; second, many native Spanish speakers consider it poor taste to mention directly one's body parts.

In English we reserve the use of the reflexive pronouns (*myself, yourself,* etc.) generally for what can be called "full-body experiences"—that is, "I love *myself*," "she sees *herself* in the full-length mirror," "they don't understand *themselves*." In Spanish, the use is much narrower: most of us wash our own hair (as opposed to the hair stylist doing this for us or our washing someone else's hair); similarly, most of us dress ourselves, comb our own hair, etc. Simply remember that if the action doesn't leave the subject/performer, it will be reflexive.

examples:

Me lavo el pelo cada día.
I wash my hair every day.

Te pesas cada mañana.
You weigh yourself every morning.

Ella **se baña** con jabón especial.
She *bathes* with special soap.

Nos afeitamos dos veces al día.
We shave twice a day.

Os cepilláis los dientes.
You brush your teeth.

Se lavan las manos.
They wash their hands.

ejercicio   I-11-1

1. I take a shower. _____

2. I take a bath. _____

3. You (*s., fam.*) take a shower every day. _____

4. He shaves every morning. _____

5. She brushes her teeth three times a day. _____

6. We brush our teeth. _____

7. They shave twice a day. _____

8. He washes his hair. _____

9. I wash my face. _____

10. You (*s., fam.*) dry your hair. _____

11. You (*s., formal*) dry yourself with a towel (*la toalla*). _____

12. I comb my hair often (*a menudo*). _____

13. She almost never (*casi nunca*) combs her hair. _____

14. I weigh myself on the bathroom scales (*la báscula de baño*). _____

15. She weighs herself twice a day. _____

What Makes a Verb Reflexive?

It is important to note that *nearly all verbs can be made reflexive*. There is nothing magical about a reflexive verb. All it means is that the action is not leaving the agent/performer. You can wash your car (nonreflexive) or you can wash your face (reflexive); you can put your child to bed (nonreflexive) or you can go to bed/put yourself to bed (reflexive).

Because most verbs can be made reflexive—in virtue of the agent performing the act on himself or herself—it is impossible to list all or even most of them here.

The verbs in the following list are usually used in the reflexive form, because of the nature of the action they represent:

acostarse (o→ue)	to go to bed
casarse (con alguien)	to get married; to marry (someone)
desmayarse	to faint
despertarse (e→ie)	to wake up
desvestirse (e→i)	to get undressed
dormirse (o→ue)	to fall asleep
enfermarse	to get/become sick
enojarse	to get/become angry
hacerse	to become (voluntarily—literally, "to make oneself")
irse	to go away
levantarse	to stand up, get up (literally, "to lift oneself")
llamarse	to call oneself; to be called
mirarse	to look at oneself
ponerse	to become (involuntarily, often emotionally)
ponerse (la ropa)	to put on (clothing)
preocuparse (de/por/con)	to worry (about)
probarse (o→ue) (la ropa)	to try on (clothing)
quedarse	to stay, remain
quitarse (la ropa)	to take off, remove (clothing)
sentarse (e→ie)	to sit down, seat oneself
sentirse (e→ie)	to feel (emotionally, physically)
verse	to see oneself
vestirse (e→i)	to dress oneself

examples:

Me quedo en un hotel de lujo.
I stay in a luxury hotel.

Te llamas Pedro.
Your name is (*You call yourself*) Pedro.

Nancy **se siente** enferma.
Nancy *feels* sick.

Nos vemos en el espejo.
We see ourselves in the mirror.

Os sentáis en los sillones.
You're sitting in the easy chairs.

Ellas **se enferman.**
They *get sick*.

¿Verdadero o falso?

_____ 1. Me enojo mucho con personas que no toman responsabilidad por sus acciones.

_____ 2. Cuando viajo a otra ciudad, siempre me quedo en un hotel de cuatro estrellas.

_____ 3. Me levanto para cenar y me siento para caminar.

_____ 4. Si veo sangre (*blood*), me pongo enfermo/a y después me desmayo.

_____ 5. Cuando me enojo con alguien, hablo con esa persona para resolver el problema.

_____ 6. Es importante ponerse manoplas (*mittens*) y una chaqueta de lana (*wool*) cuando hace mucho frío.

_____ 7. Siempre me quito los zapatos antes de entrar en la casa.

_____ 8. Muchas personas se ponen muy furiosas cuando conducen en las autopistas.

_____ 9. El presidente de la nación se llama Günther.

_____ 10. Cuando una persona se casa con otra persona, esta ceremonia se llama la boda.

_____ 11. Cuando una persona se queda en un hotel de lujo, normalmente se siente muy elegante.

_____ 12. Una persona puede hacerse millonaria si trabaja quince horas al día durante veinte años.

ejercicio   I-11-2

1. When I try on clothing, I look at myself in the mirror. _____

_____

2. What time (*a qué hora*) do you (*s., fam.*) go to bed and what time do you get up? _____

_____

3. Normally people get married on (*durante*) the weekends. _____

_____

4. I get sick when I eat food that has a lot of fat (*la grasa*). _____

_____

5. I go (*away*) to work (*al trabajo*) every morning at eight o'clock. _____

_____

6. I take a shower, I brush my teeth, I dry my hair, I get dressed, and then I go to work. _____

_____

7. I become (*involuntarily*) sick when I see a hair (*el pelo*) in (*the*) food. _____

_____

8. Miss America faints when she puts on the crown (*la corona*). _____

   _____

9. Every night I get undressed, I put on my pajamas (*el pijama*), I go to bed, and I fall asleep.

   _____

10. When Laura stays in a hotel, she worries about the safety (*la seguridad*) of her family. _____

   _____

Preposition + Infinitive with the Reflexive Object Pronoun

Any verb that directly follows a preposition must remain in the infinitive. With reflexive verbs, the infinitive stays untouched; however, the reflexive pronoun changes to agree with the stated or understood subject. This pronoun is attached directly to the infinitive. You can usually determine the subject of the reflexive verb through the context of the sentence.

examples:

Yo leo **antes de acostarme.**
I read *before going to bed.*

Cenamos **después de lavarnos** las manos.
We eat dinner *after washing* our hands.

Después de quitarse las botas, él entra en la casa.
After taking off his boots, he enters the house.

Antes de dormirse, ellos cuentan ovejas.
Before falling asleep, they count sheep.

En vez de acostarme, voy a quedarme despierto toda la noche.
Instead of going to bed, I'm going to stay awake all night long.

ejercicio   I-11-3

Fill in the blank with the appropriate reflexive pronoun.

1. Antes de vestir_____, yo plancho (*iron*) la ropa.

2. Después de bañar_____, Mariana se acuesta.

3. Antes de ir_____ al trabajo, leemos el periódico.

4. Después de levantar_____, hago la cama.

5. Ellos cenan después de sentar_____.

6. Dorian Gray grita con horror después de ver_____ en el retrato (*portrait*).

7. Después de probar_____ diez vestidos y veinte trajes de baño, Cathy se frustra mucho.

8. Antes de acostar_____, siempre me cepillo los dientes.

9. Antes de afeitar_____, preparas la crema de afeitar.

10. Después de vestir_____, salís para el trabajo.

11. Necesito champú para lavar_____ el pelo.

12. Ella va a bañar_____ en vez de duchar_____ hoy.

ejercicio   I-11-4

1. After getting dressed, I look at myself in the mirror.

   _____

2. Before going away, we put on our (*the*) coats (*el abrigo*), mittens (*la manopla*), and hats.

   _____

3. After taking a bath, I put on my robe (*la bata*) and I relax (*relajarse*).

   _____

4. Instead of (*en vez de*) taking a shower, I'm going to take a bath tonight.

   _____

5. This soap is the best for (*para*) washing your (*s., formal*) face.

   _____

6. I use this shampoo (*el champú*) for washing my hair.

   _____

7. When I stay in a hotel, I always request a call (*la llamada*) to (*para*) wake me up.

   _____

8. He takes a pill (*la pastilla*) every night in order to (*para*) fall asleep.

   _____

9. Some people meditate (*meditar*) in order to relax.

   _____

10. You (*pl., fam.*) need a razor (*la navaja*) and a blade (*la hoja*) in order to shave (*yourselves*).

   _____

When the Second Verb Is Reflexive

In sentences with two verbs that act upon one another, as always, you conjugate the first verb and leave the second in the infinitive. When that second verb is reflexive, attach the appropriate reflexive pronoun directly to the infinitive.

examples:

Necesito **lavarme** el pelo.
I need *to wash* my hair.

¿Cuándo vas a **acostarte?**
When are you going *to go to bed?*

Ella no puede **verse** en el cristal.
She can't *see herself* in the glass.

Tenemos que **irnos** ahora.
We have *to leave* now.

Debéis **quitaros** los zapatos.
You should *take off* your shoes.

¿Quieren ustedes **quedarse** aquí?
Do you want *to stay* here?

¿Verdadero o falso?

_____ 1. Esta noche voy a acostarme a las once y media.

_____ 2. Durante la semana tengo que levantarme antes de las siete de la mañana.

_____ 3. Debo cepillarme los dientes por lo menos tres veces al día.

_____ 4. Me gusta quedarme en hoteles cuando visito otras ciudades.

_____ 5. Prefiero probarme ropa nueva en mi casa y no en el probador (*fitting room*) de una tienda.

_____ 6. Me molesta ponerme tanta ropa en el invierno.

_____ 7. Quiero enfermarme mucho este año.

_____ 8. Quiero casarme con una persona famosa y tener fotos de nuestra boda en el *Enquirer.*

_____ 9. Cuando no puedo dormirme, leo.

_____ 10. Si no tengo tiempo para ducharme en la mañana, me siento sucio/a e incómodo/a todo el día.

_____ 11. No me gusta irme al trabajo sin tomar café primero.

_____ 12. Muchas personas quieren hacerse ricas algún día.

_____ 13. Una persona tiene que quitarse la ropa antes de bañarse.

_____ 14. Muchas personas prefieren quedarse en un Motel 6 para ahorrar dinero.

_____ 15. Nadie quiere quedarse en un hotel con ratones, ratas, arañas y todo tipo de insectos.

ejercicio   I-11-5

1. For our honeymoon (*la luna de miel*), we want to stay in an elegant hotel. _____
   _____

2. Where are you (*pl., formal*) going to stay in Paris? _____
   _____

3. I am very warm. I'm going to take off my sweater. _____
   _____

4. I am very cold. I have to put on my coat. _____

5. No one wants to get sick, but unfortunately (*desgraciadamente*) this happens (*ocurrir*). _____
   _____

6. Our dog likes to bathe himself in our neighbor's swimming pool. _____
   _____

7. If you (*s., fam.*) want to wash your hair, there is shampoo in the cabinet (*el gabinete*). _____
   _____

8. If you (*s., formal*) want to shave, the concierge (*el conserje*) can give you a razor (*la navaja*) and
   some blades (*la hoja*).
   _____

9. If you (*pl., formal*) want to get well (*bien*), you have to eat (*tomar*) this chicken soup (*el caldo de pollo*).
   _____

10. You (*s., fam.*) are going to get sick if you eat that raw (*crudo*) meat. _____
    _____

traducción   I-11-6

"He never bathes anymore! It's absolutely terrible." My neighbor tells me everything, and today she is complaining about her husband. She is a fastidious woman and complains all the time. She tells me that I should wash my hair more often. I tell her that that is my problem and that she should be quiet. She tells me that she can't be quiet when no one in her family bathes or showers. She tells me that after going to bed, she can't fall asleep because she's worrying about all these people who don't wash themselves. I tell her that she can buy herself either a can of Lysol or a hose.

vocabulario

(aerosol) can	**el bote**	either . . . or	**o . . . o**
anymore	**ya**	fastidious	**fastidioso/a**
(to) be quiet	**callarse**	hose	**la manguera**
(to) complain about	**quejarse de**	more often	**más a menudo**

_____

_____

_____

_____

_____

_____

_____

_____

_____

_____

_____

_____

_____

_____

_____

_____

_____

_____

_____

_____

RID: Sentences with Two Object Pronouns

FUNCTION: Provides standard syntax when there are two object pronouns in a sentence

SPANISH PLACEMENT: Either directly preceding the first (conjugated) verb or attached directly to the second (infinitive) verb: always in the order reflexive, indirect, direct

ENGLISH EQUIVALENTS: (See examples throughout the unit.)

The following chart is a review of the reflexive, indirect, and direct object pronouns.

Reflexive Pronouns		Indirect Object Pronouns		Direct Object Pronouns	
me	nos	me	nos	me	nos
te	os	te	os	te	os
se	se	le	les	lo/la	los/las

The RID Order

When you have two object pronouns in a sentence, these pronouns always will appear in the RID order: *reflexive, indirect, direct* object pronouns. Because two is the maximum number of pronouns that can appear together, the possible combinations are reflexive-indirect (rare), reflexive-direct, or indirect-direct.

examples:

Reflexive-Direct

Me lo compro.
I buy *it for myself.*

Tu pelo es magnífico. ¿**Te lo** lavas mucho?
Your hair is wonderful. Do *you* wash *it* a lot?

Indirect-Direct

Ellos **os los** envían.
They send *them to you.*

Yo **te la** escribo.
I write *it to you.*

Ella **me las** vende.
She sells *them to me.*

ejercicio   I-12-1

*Unless marked (f.), it and **them** are masculine. You = second-person familiar.*

1. He gives it to me. _____

2. She tells it to you. _____

3. We give it to you. _____

4. I write it (f.) to you. _____

5. He sends them to us. _____

6. We sing it (f.) to you. _____

7. Why do you give it to me? _____

8. Who has it for you? _____

9. When do you do it for me? _____

10. Why do you tell it to us? _____

11. I prepare it (f.) for myself. _____

12. She buys them (f.) for herself. _____

The *La La* Rule

When both the direct and the indirect objects are in the third person, both pronouns, regardless of number or gender, will begin with the letter *l*. When this happens, change the indirect object pronoun (the first one) to **se.** The reason for this is to avoid the singsong, tongue-tripping quality of the two small words starting with the letter *l.* We call this the "la la rule."

Consider the sentence "I give it (*m.*) to him." The indirect object is *him* (**le**) and the direct object is *it* (**lo**). Thus we first have **Yo *le lo* doy.** Because of the *la la* rule, we will change the indirect object **le** to **se,** and the result will be **Yo *se lo* doy.**

Remember: We use pronouns only when their antecedents are understood from the context of the paragraph or conversation. So, while looking at **Se lo doy** without any prior knowledge makes the sentence virtually meaningless, knowledge of the referents makes the sentence completely understandable.

examples:

Tú conoces a Juan. Mejor **se lo** dices tú.
You know Juan. It's better if you tell *it to him.*

Tenemos muchos lápices que no necesitamos. **Se los** damos.
We have a lot of pencils we don't need. We give *them to you (s., formal).*

Los padres de Enrique lo miman. Si él quiere una bicicleta, ellos **se la** compran.
Enrique's parents spoil him. If he wants a bicycle, they buy *it for him.*

A mi mamá le fascinan los chocolates. Por eso, **se los** envío.
My mother loves chocolates. That's why I send *them to her.*

ejercicio	I-12-2

Unless marked (f.), it *and* **them** *are masculine. You = second-person familiar, unless otherwise indicated.*

1. He sings it (*f.*) to her. _____

2. We tell it to them. _____

3. You buy them for him. _____

4. I write it for you (*pl., formal*). _____

5. He sends them to them. _____

6. I tell it to her. _____

7. He sells it (*f.*) to her. _____

8. You give them (*f.*) to him. _____

9. No one tells it to her. _____

10. Why do you tell it to him? _____

11. We bring them (*f.*) to them (*f.*). _____

12. She cooks it for them. _____

13. I make them (*f.*) for you (*pl., formal*). _____

14. Do you make them for them? _____

15. Who gives it to them? _____

Two Pronouns in a Negative Statement

In a negative sentence or clause in which the **RID** rules apply, place the word **no** (or other word of negation) directly before the first pronoun. Note the *la la* rule in action in the examples, and watch for sentences like them in the exercises that follow.

examples:

No te lo tengo.   **No se los** tengo.
I do*n't* have *it for you.*   I do*n't* have *them for them.*

Nunca se la compran.   **No nos las** vendemos.
They *never* buy *it for her.*   We do*n't* sell *them to ourselves.*

ejercicio   I-12-3

*Unless marked (f.), **it** and **them** are masculine. You = second-person familiar, unless otherwise indicated.*

1. She doesn't tell it to me. _____

2. I don't tell it to him. _____

3. We don't buy them (f.) for ourselves. _____

4. They don't send it (f.) to us on time (*a tiempo*). _____

5. She doesn't make it for us every day. _____

6. I don't give it (f.) to them. _____

7. He doesn't pay me for it in cash (*en efectivo*). _____

8. He doesn't give it to me on time. _____

9. Why don't you send it (f.) to her tomorrow? _____

10. Don't you buy them (f.) for them every day? _____

11. I never buy them for myself. _____

12. We never tell them to her. _____

RID in Sentences with Two Verbs

In sentences that contain two verbs, the RID pronoun rule still applies; however, now you will attach both pronouns directly to the second verb—namely, the infinitive. You have seen this same syntactic rule with each of the individual pronouns.

In order to retain the natural accent of the infinitive (the second verb), which always falls on the final syllable, you now add an accent mark over the vowel in that syllable: **comer + se + lo = *comérselo*; entregar + me + las = *entregármelas*; vender + nos + los = *vendérnoslos*.**

You can also, if you choose, place the two pronouns before the first, conjugated verb. In that case, there will be no need to add an accent to the final syllable of the infinitive: **se lo puede comer; me las quiere entregar; nos los debe vender.**

examples:

Quiero **dártelo.**
Te lo quiero **dar.**
I want *to give it to you.*

Tienes que **enviármela.**
Me la tienes que **enviar.**
You have *to send it to me.*

Ella puede **hacérselo.**
Ella **se lo** puede **hacer.**
She can *do it for herself.*

Queremos **decírselo.**
Se lo queremos **decir.**
We want *to say it to him.*

Necesitáis **ponéroslo.**
Os lo necesitáis **poner.**
You need *to put it on yourselves.*

Ustedes pueden **escondérnoslo.**
Ustedes **nos lo** pueden **esconder.**
You can *hide it from us.*

| ejercicio | I-12-4 |

*Express each of the following statements in two ways. Unless marked (f.), **it** and **them** are masculine. You = second-person familiar, unless otherwise indicated.*

1. I want to tell it to you. _____

2. I want to buy it (*f.*) for you. _____

3. You have to give it to me. _____

4. We have to sell them to you. _____

5. We have to sell it to her. _____

6. They should buy them (*f.*) for you. _____

7. They should buy it for themselves. _____

8. She needs to send it (*f.*) to me. _____

9. You (*pl., formal*) have to give it (*f.*) to us. _____

10. I should bring it to them. _____

11. They should bring them (*f.*) to me. _____

12. She wants to sing it (*f.*) for us. _____

13. You can send it to me by mail (*por correo*). _____

14. He can pay you for it (*f.*) in cash. _____

15. I want to pay you (*pl., fam.*) for them by check (*con un cheque*). _____

Questions and Negative Statements with Two Verbs

In a negative sentence with two verbs, place the word **no** (or other word of negation) directly before the first, conjugated verb. If you choose to place the pronouns before the conjugated verb, the word **no** will precede the pronouns.

For questions, just add question marks. If you want to add the subject's name or pronoun, do so after the first, conjugated verb.

examples:

No quiero **dejártelo.**   No tenemos que **comprárselo.**
No **te lo** quiero **dejar.**   No **se lo** tenemos que **comprar.**
I don't want *to leave it for you.*   We don't have *to buy it for him.*

¿Quieres **dejármelo?**
¿Me lo quieres **dejar?**
Do you want *to leave it for me?*

¿Podéis **escribírmelo?**
¿Me lo podéis **escribir?**
Can you *write it for me?*

¿Marcos no necesita **regalárselo?**
¿Marcos no **se lo** necesita **regalar?**
Doesn't Marcos need *to give it to her?*

Ellos nunca saben **decírselo.**
Ellos nunca **se lo** saben **decir.**
They never know how *to tell it to her.*

ejercicio   I-12-5

*Express each of the following statements in two ways. Unless marked (**f.**), it and **them** are masculine. You = second-person familiar, unless otherwise indicated.*

1. Can you do it for me? _____

2. No, I can't do it for you. _____

3. Do we have to tell it (*f.*) to him? _____

4. When do you want to give them (*f.*) to them? _____

5. You don't need to pay me for it now. _____

6. They can't sell it to you in the United States. _____

7. We can't sell it (*f.*) to them at this price. _____

8. When do you want to tell it to me? _____

9. Aren't you going to bring it to us today? _____

10. Can't they send them (*f.*) to us by mail (*por correo*)? _____

_____

traducción   I-12-6

Every year I receive lots of presents for my birthday. I have lots of friends who have stores, and they always give me what they sell or what they make. And for their birthdays, I always give them presents too. My friend Merlin sells flowers, and he gives them to me. Manolo sells shoes, and he gives me them. Juan sells coffee, and he gives it to me. Vidal sells shampoo, and he gives it to me. Paloma makes perfume, and she sends it to me because she lives in Spain. Donna makes dresses, and she sends them to me. Elsa makes jewelry, and she always makes something for my birthday. This year I want a private jet. Who is going to give it to me?

vocabulario

flowers	**las flores**	perfume	**el perfume**
(to) give (a gift)	**regalar**	private jet	**el avión privado**
jewelry	**las joyas**	something	**algo**

_____

_____

_____

_____

_____

_____

_____

_____

_____

_____

_____

_____

_____

_____

_____

_____

_____

_____

_____

Reciprocal Pronouns

The term *reciprocity* indicates that whatever is going on is happening equally between or among all the interested parties. If I see you, but you don't see me, there is no reciprocity. However, when we see each other, reciprocity takes place.

Since reciprocity can occur only when two or more persons are involved, the reciprocal pronouns exist only in the plural forms. Thus, the phrase *each other* or *one another* will figure in the sentences involving reciprocal pronouns.

> **nos** (ourselves: each other, one another)
> **os** (yourselves: each other, one another)
> **se** (themselves; yourselves: each other, one another)

As you can see in the chart, the reciprocal pronouns are the same as the reflexive pronouns. All the rules of syntax that apply to direct, indirect, and reflexive pronouns also apply to reciprocal pronouns.

examples:

Nos vemos cada día.
We see each other every day.

¿Os conocéis bien?
Do you know each other well?

Ellos **no pueden escribirse** muy a menudo.
They *can't write to one another* very often.

Siempre **nos encontramos** en el supermercado pero **nunca nos hablamos.**
We always *run into one another* at the supermarket, but *we never speak to each other.*

ejercicio I-13-1

Fill in each blank with the appropriate reciprocal pronoun (the conjugated verb will give provide you the clue). Then translate the sentence into English.

1. _____ conocemos muy bien.

   _____

2. Ellos _____ quieren mucho.

   _____

3. _____ veis por la ventana.

   _____

4. ¿_____ conocen ustedes?

   _____

5. _____ besan cada mañana.

   _____

6. Cada día _____ decimos "te quiero".

   _____

7. Cuando ellos están enojados, no _____ hablan.

   _____

8. ¿_____ visitáis con frecuencia?

   _____

9. Ellos _____ pelean (*fight*) mucho porque _____ odian.

   _____

10. _____ hablamos por teléfono tres veces cada semana.

    _____

11. Ellos quieren conocer_____ mejor.

    _____

12. No podemos ver_____ tan a menudo como queremos.

    _____

ejercicio   I-13-2

1. We write long letters to each other every week. _____

2. When do you (*pl., fam.*) see each other? _____

3. Why do they yell at (*gritar*) each other so much? _____

4. The lovebirds (*los tórtolos*) sing to one another in the treetop (*la copa del árbol*). _____

_____

5. We buy each other gifts every December. _____

6. They run into each other at the gym (*el gimnasio*) every Friday afternoon. _____

_____

7. We can't speak to each other because my telephone doesn't work (*funcionar*). _____

_____

8. You (*pl., formal*) shouldn't tell each other everything. He can't keep (*guardar*) a secret. _____

_____

9. You (*pl., fam.*) can look at each other now. _____

10. My neighbors yell at one another every Saturday night. _____

_____

traducción   I-13-3

I'm going to my high school reunion in two weeks. I'm very excited because Henry is going to attend. I know this because Laura, my best friend, is the secretary of the class. She and I talk to each other every week, and she tells me everything. These reunions are tricky. We want to see one another, but at the same time we don't want to see one another. Or, maybe, we want to see each other in the past, which doesn't exist anymore. Some people see each other after many years, and it is wonderful. But there are other people who see each other, and it isn't wonderful.

vocabulario

at the same time	**al mismo tiempo**	maybe	**tal vez**
(to) attend	**asistir**	not . . . anymore	**ya no** + *conjugated verb*
excited	**ilusionado/a**	reunion	**la reunión**
(to) exist	**existir**	tricky	**delicado/a**
high school	**la escuela secundaria**	which	**lo cual**

_____

_____

_____

_____

_____

_____

_____

_____

_____

_____

_____

_____

_____

_____

_____

_____

_____

_____

_____

Se and the Passive Voice

The Passive Voice

We use the passive voice to describe an action that is carried out but has no specific, identified agent. For example, in the sentence, "The doors are unlocked at 5:30," there is no identified subject or agent. We don't know *who* actually unlocks the doors. See the following examples that contrast the active and the passive voices.

Active Voice	Passive Voice
Paul *closes* the shop at 9:00.	The shop *is closed* at 9:00.
Sue *heard* a baby crying.	A baby's cries *were heard*.
The wind *blew* down the tree.	The tree *was blown* down.

Each sentence in the active voice has a specific subject, but the corresponding sentence in the passive voice has an unspecified subject—we don't know *who* closes the shop, *who* heard the baby's cries, or *what* blew down the tree.

There are basically two ways to express the passive voice in Spanish: (1) by using a form of **ser** and a participle and (2) by using **se** and a conjugated form of the verb.

Joaquín **es respetado.**	La fortaleza **fue destruida.**
Se respeta a Joaquín.	La fortaleza **se destruyó.**
Joaquín *is respected.*	The fortress *was destroyed.*

In both examples, the passive voice expresses the result of an action, but not the agent, or performer, of the action.

Formation of the Passive Voice with *se*

To use **se** as a substitute for the passive voice in Spanish, place **se** before the conjugated verb in the third person. If the noun following the verb is singular, you will conjugate the verb in the third-person singular; if that noun is plural or if there is a series of nouns, you will conjugate the verb in the third-person plural.

Se habla español en México.	**Se hablan** inglés y francés en Canadá.
Spanish *is spoken* in Mexico.	English and French *are spoken* in Canada.

Se vende plata en esta joyería.
Silver *is sold* at this jewelry store.

No **se venden** joyas aquí.
Jewels *are* not *sold* here.

Las historietas no **se consideran** obras literarias.
Comic books *are* not *considered* literary works.

ejercicio   I-14-1

Fill in the appropriate form of the verb given in parentheses.

1. Se (*vender*) _____ ropa en Bloomingdale's.

2. Se (*comer*) _____ mucho pescado en Japón.

3. Se (*hacer*) _____ películas en Hollywood.

4. Se (*bailar*) _____ la rumba y el mambo en Cuba.

5. Se (*cultivar*) _____ café y azúcar en El Salvador.

6. Se (*exportar*) _____ oro, azúcar, café y níquel de la República Dominicana.

7. Se (*bailar*) _____ flamenco en España.

8. Se (*fabricar*) _____ coches en Detroit.

9. Se (*limar*) [*file*] _____ las uñas en el salón de belleza.

10. Se (*fabricar*) _____ papel en el noroeste de los Estados Unidos.

ejercicio   I-14-2

1. Spanish is spoken here. _____

2. Spanish and French are spoken here. _____

3. Shoes are sold there. _____

4. Fireworks (*los fuegos artificiales*) are not sold to teenagers (*el adolescente*). _____

5. Entrance (*la entrada*) is not permitted (*permitir*) before 10:00. _____

6. Cameras are not permitted in the theater. _____

7. Gold and jewels are not considered good investments (*la inversión*). _____

_____

8. The stores and the museums are closed on Tuesdays. _____

_____

9. The bank is closed at two-thirty. _____

10. Piñatas are made (*fabricar*) in this factory (*la fábrica*). _____

_____

Using *se* to Avoid the Passive

In Spanish as in English, overuse of the passive voice creates boring conversation and prose. One way to avoid the passive is to use an impersonal subject. For example, in "They dance the cumbia in Colombia," we don't know specifically who *they* are; there are no names or faces attached. The subject refers to many people in general, but no one in particular.

In English, another common impersonal subject is the word *you*, as in "You shouldn't call me after nine." Other common impersonal subjects in English include *it, they, one, people, anybody,* and *no one.*

No se debe matar.
One shouldn't kill.
You shouldn't kill.

¡Así **se hace!**
That's how *it's done!*
That's how *you do it!*

¿Qué **se puede hacer?**
What's *a person to do?*
What *can you do?*

Jamás se explicó el asesinato.
They never explained the murder.
No one ever explained the murder.

En este club **se baila** la cumbia y el mambo, pero no la Macarena.
In this club *they dance* the cumbia and the mambo, but not the Macarena.
In this club *people dance* the cumbia and the mambo, but not the Macarena.

Notice in these examples that when an impersonal subject is intended, the third-person singular is used. However, often when the plural is used to express the same idea, the reflexive **se** is dropped.

Se me conoce aquí.
Me conocen aquí.
They know me here.

Aquí **se produce** el mejor café.
Aquí **producen** el mejor café.
They produce the best coffee here.

Se dice que **no se puede** fumar en ninguna parte.
Dicen que **no se puede** fumar en ninguna parte.
They say that *you can't* smoke anywhere.

Note: When working with a reflexive verb, the reflexive action is understood through the use of **se.** Note also that most platitudes employ the passive voice (as in the second example below).

Se debe bañar cada día.
One should bathe every day.

Se puede dirigir el caballo al agua . . .
You can lead a horse to water . . .

No se puede tomar esta ruta.
You can't take this route.

Se puede comer y beber en esta sala.
We can eat and drink in this room.

Aquí **se prohíbe** sacar fotos.   No **se tiene** que tolerar tal crueldad.
It is forbidden to take pictures here.   *One doesn't have* to tolerate such cruelty.

ejercicio   I-14-3

1. You should pay your taxes (*los impuestos*) every April. _____

    _____

2. You can't be in two places at the same time (*al mismo tiempo*). _____

    _____

3. You need to change the oil (*el aceite*) in your car every (*cada*) three thousand miles. _____

    _____

4. One shouldn't blame (*culpar*) others for the results (*el resultado*) of his/her actions. _____

    _____

5. One should exercise (*hacer ejercicio*) and meditate (*meditar*) daily. _____

    _____

6. They should make these maps clearer. You can't read this! _____

    _____

7. You can't get (*extraer*) blood from a turnip (*el nabo*). _____

    _____

8. You can't judge (*juzgar*) a book by its cover (*la portada*). _____

    _____

9. People should brush their teeth after (*después de*) eating. _____

    _____

10. You can swim and play tennis in this club. _____

11. In order to dance La Bamba, you need a little bit of grace (*una poca de gracia*). _____

    _____

12. They never explained the UFOs (*los OVNIs*). _____

13. Can one go in (*entrar*)? _____

14. In this store, people pay a fixed price (*un precio fijo*). _____

_____

15. It is said that you should look before (*antes de*) you leap (*saltar*). _____

_____

The Passive Voice with Inanimate Objects

We often speak of actions that take place in which there is no—at least no apparent—human element involved in the action, for example, "My car breaks down on me every winter." We also often refer to actions that clearly are performed by humans, but for which the mention of those humans is irrelevant, for example, "The store opens at 10:00."

In these situations, we use the passive voice, which allows us to focus on the action and completely ignore the performer of the action. Just remember that if the noun is singular, use the singular form of the verb; if the noun is plural, use the plural form.

Note: The object can either precede or follow the verb.

examples:

Se abre la tienda a las diez.
La tienda se abre a las diez.
The store opens at ten.

Se abren las tiendas a las diez.
Las tiendas se abren a las diez.
The stores open at ten.

Se estropea mi coche cada invierno.
Mi coche se estropea cada invierno.
My car breaks down every winter.

Se arreglan los pantalones en esta sastrería.
Los pantalones se arreglan en esta sastrería.
Pants are fixed in this tailor's shop.

ejercicio   I-14-4

1. The mall (*el centro comercial*) closes at nine-thirty. _____

_____

2. I get angry when I pay seven dollars to see a movie, and the projector (*el proyector*) breaks down

(*descomponerse*). _____

3. Lightbulbs (*la bombilla*) usually burn out (*quemarse*) after one hundred hours. _____

_____

4. When a car breaks down (*estropearse*) on the freeway (*la autopista*), it's a catastrophe (*el catástrofe*)

for everyone. _____

5. What time does that restaurant open? _____

6. The sun sets (*ponerse*) at eight-thirty P.M. in the summer. _____

_____

7. With this appliance (*el aparato*), your lights turn on (*encenderse*) and turn off (*apagarse*) automatically

(*automáticamente*). _____

8. After the holidays (*los días de fiesta*), millions of toys break (*romperse*). _____

_____

9. When she sings, all the glasses break (*quebrarse* [*e→ie*]). _____

_____

10. The museums close at six sharp (*en punto*). _____

traducción   I-14-5

I want to go to Madrid for my next vacation. I have a brochure with me now. Let's see! What can a person do in Madrid? They say here that the Prado is one of the world's greatest museums and that you can spend several days exploring its treasures. It says that in Madrid the subway system is very good, so one doesn't need to rent a car. You can take the subway to all the sites in the city. If you go to a good restaurant in Madrid, you can try roast piglet. Also, El Retiro is a lovely park, and people can rent little boats to go around the pond. You can attend the bullfights, and you can dance until five o'clock in the morning. You can do everything in this marvelous city!

vocabulario

(to) attend	**asistir a**	(to) rent	**alquilar**
(little) boat	**el barquito**	pond	**el estanque**
brochure	**el folleto**	roast piglet	**el cochinillo asado**
bullfight	**la corrida**	several	**varios/as**
everything	**de todo**	site	**el sitio**
(to) go around	**recorrer**	so	**así que**
greatest (*pl.*)	**mejores**	(to) spend (time)	**pasar**
Let's see	**A ver**	subway	**el metro**
lovely	**precioso/a**	system	**el sistema**
marvelous	**maravilloso/a**	treasure	**el tesoro**
museum	**el museo**	(to) try	**probar (o→ue)**
next	**próximo/a**	vacation	**las vacaciones**

PART II

Prepositions

Prepositions (and Related Terms)

What is a preposition? A preposition is the part of speech that shows the relation of a noun or a pronoun to some other word in a sentence, clause, or phrase.

Prepositions often are referred to as "those little words." But they are little words that mean a lot, for prepositions reveal place, time, direction, manner, and companionship, among other things.

For the most part, prepositions are used to show the relationship between nouns and pronouns.

I am *with* Carlota.	Roberto is *near* my house.
Estoy **con** Carlota.	Roberto está **cerca de** mi casa.
You are *in* the hospital?	The cat is *on top of* the bookshelf.
¿Estás **en** el hospital?	El gato está **encima del** estante.

Each of the prepositions used in the examples reveals the relationship between the subject of the sentence (I, Roberto, you, cat) and the object of the preposition (Carlota, house, hospital, bookshelf). To change a preposition is to change the meaning of the sentence entirely.

I am *far from* Carlota.	Roberto is *in* my house.
Estoy **lejos de** Carlota.	Roberto está **en** mi casa.
You are *next door to* the hospital?	The cat is *behind* the bookshelf.
¿Estás **al lado del** hospital?	El gato está **detrás del** estante.

Because prepositions are so specific in meaning, it is important to study them in depth. As a rule, you cannot substitute or "talk around" these words; prepositions do not have synonyms the way many nouns and other words do. The language blossoms for the student who has a command of prepositions.

Prepositions or Adverbs?

The relationship between nouns and pronouns in a sentence is revealed by prepositions. Other than the preposition itself, their only link is a verb, usually the verb *to be.* In the previous examples, you'll find I *am,* Roberto *is,* you *are,* the cat *is.*

At times, however, these prepositions actually modify a verb. While the term or prepositional phrase itself does not change, its part of speech does. That is, its function in the sentence changes from preposition to adverb. Here is the guideline:

The term is a preposition if it connects two (or more) nouns and/or pronouns. In these cases, the verb will almost always be the linking verb *to be.* In Spanish, depending on the context, the linking verb will be **ser** or **estar.**

The same term or prepositional phrase becomes an adverb when, instead of linking nouns or pronouns, it modifies an action verb.

Linking Verb—Preposition

El ladrón **está cerca de** la casa.
The thief *is near* the house.

John **está detrás de** la pared.
John *is behind* the wall.

Action Verb—Adverb

El ladrón **se esconde cerca de** la casa.
The thief *is hiding near* the house.

John **camina detrás de** la pared.
John *walks behind* the wall.

The next section of the text essentially is intended to build your vocabulary. Take the time to learn these words and terms well. An ability to work—and play—with them will increase your command of the Spanish language enormously.

Prepositions Showing a Relationship Between Nouns and/or Pronouns

One of the principal functions of a preposition is to demonstrate what the connection or relationship is between two or more people or things. This relationship can be physical and concrete, as in "The chair is *against* the wall"; or it can be abstract, as in "He writes poems *about* love."

examples:

La silla está **contra** la pared.
The chair is *against* the wall.

Quiero un libro **sobre** economía.
I want a book *on* economics.

Escribe poemas **acerca** del amor.
He writes poems *about* love.

Además de tacos, Lola prepara la salsa.
In addition to tacos, Lola prepares the salsa.

The following list contains prepositions that show a relationship. They are used in the exercises that follow.

about	**acerca de**
about, on (topic)	**sobre**
according to	**según**
against	**contra**
besides, in addition to	**además de**
except	**excepto, menos, salvo**
instead of	**en vez de, en lugar de**
with	**con**
without	**sin**

¿Verdadero o falso?

_____ 1. Yo sé mucho acerca de Hollywood.

_____ 2. Me gusta el té con limón y azúcar.

_____ 3. En la Serie Mundial, la Liga Nacional juega contra la Liga Americana.

_____ 4. Según mi mejor amigo/a, un día sin café es un día sin valor.

_____ 5. Yo como todo tipo de comida, excepto chocolate.

_____ 6. Aristóteles escribió ensayos sobre filosofía.

_____ 7. Yo estudio matemáticas además de español.

_____ 8. Según la Biblia, Adán y Eva fueron las primeras personas del mundo.

_____ 9. Siempre dejo mis zapatos contra la pared.

_____ 10. Tengo un libro sobre la historia de Francia.

_____ 11. Me gusta oír noticias acerca de mis amigos.

_____ 12. Además de ropa, Bloomingdale's vende muebles, coches y refrigeradores.

_____ 13. Yo soy una persona sin problemas.

_____ 14. Nadie, menos los niños pequeños, cree que existe Santa Claus.

_____ 15. En este momento estoy con mi mejor amigo/a.

_____ 16. Tomo té en vez de café.

ejercicio   II-1-1

*In this exercise, you = second-person singular (**tú**).*

1. He always talks about his girlfriend. _____

2. I prefer coffee with milk and sugar. _____

3. He prefers tea without sugar. _____

4. *Don Quijote* is the best novel in the world, according to José. _____

_____

5. In addition to flowers, her boyfriend gives her candy (*los dulces*) on every date (*la cita*). _____

_____

6. The director's back (*la espalda*) is against the wall. _____

7. This book is about George Washington. _____

8. They don't write much about their problems. _____

9. Do you want pizza with meat (*la carne*) or without meat? _____

10. I like everything here except the shoes. _____

11. His thesis (*la tesis*) is about the art of Rome. _____

12. According to Julia, her friends know nothing about classical music. _____

_____

13. I want everything against the wall, except the podium (*el podio*). _____

_____

14. You have to serve the drinks (*la bebida*) in addition to the food. _____

_____

15. The library doesn't have anything on (*about*) the history of the pizza. _____

_____

Prepositions of Physical Location

Perhaps the most common role of the preposition is to tell where something or someone is physically in relation to something or someone else: "The car is *in front of* the house." "John is *to the right* of Carmen."

You may notice that several prepositions of physical location are made up of more than one word. For prepositions that end with **de,** a noun or a pronoun must follow. If what is meant to follow is obvious or understood and you want to omit it, then you omit the word **de** as well and place the preposition at the end of the sentence.

El coche está **delante de** la casa.
The car is *in front of* the house.

El coche está **delante.**
The car is *in front.*

Juan está **a la derecha de** Carmen.
Juan is *to the right of* Carmen.

Juan está **a la derecha.**
Juan is *to the right.*

Estacioné el auto **enfrente del** parque.
I parked the car *across from* the park.

Estacioné el auto **enfrente.**
I parked the car *across.*

Note also that because these prepositions show location, the verb **estar** is frequently used.

The one exception to **estar** and location is when you are telling where an event takes place. In this context, you use **ser.**

Location	**Event**
María **está en** el teatro.	El concierto **es en** el teatro.
María *is in* the theater.	The concert *is in* (*at*) the theater.

At versus in: An important distinction must be made between the prepositions *at* and *in*. A good rule to remember is that prepositions in Spanish are very literal. Whereas in English you would probably say "I work *at* Sears," the reality is that when you are working, you are physically *in* Sears. Thus, you would say in Spanish, **"Trabajo *en* Sears."**

When there is no movement, you still use **en,** even though you would clearly use *at* in English.

Estoy **en** la puerta de su casa.	Estoy **en** su casa.
I am *at* the door of his house.	I am *in* (*inside*) his house.
Miro las vitrinas **en** Bloomingdale's.	Compro mi ropa **en** Bloomingdale's.
I look at the store windows *at* Bloomingdale's.	I buy my clothing *at* (*in*) Bloomingdale's.

The following are a sampling of prepositions of physical location:

above	**sobre**
across	**a través de**
across from, opposite	**enfrente de**
among	**entre (varias cosas o personas)**
at	**a, en**
behind	**detrás de**
between	**entre (dos cosas o personas)**
by	**cerca de, junto a**
facing	**frente a**
far from	**lejos de**
in	**en**
in front (of)	**delante (de)**
inside	**dentro de**
near, close to	**cerca de**
next to, next door (to)	**al lado (de), junto (a)**
on	**en**
on top of	**encima de, sobre**
outside	**fuera de**
to the left (of)	**a la izquierda (de)**
to the right (of)	**a la derecha (de)**
under	**debajo de**
with	**con**

¿Verdadero o falso?

_____   1. Hay un árbol delante de mi casa.

_____   2. En mi sala, hay una lámpara a la izquierda del sofá.

_____   3. Mi coche está dentro del garaje ahora.

_____   4. Hay una luz sobre la mesa en el comedor.

_____   5. Hay mucho polvo (*dust*) debajo de mi cama.

_____ 6. Alguien está a la derecha de mí ahora.

_____ 7. Hay un farol (*streetlight*) fuera de mi ventana.

_____ 8. Vivo cerca de una biblioteca pública.

_____ 9. El garaje está detrás de mi casa.

_____ 10. Mi mejor amigo/a vive enfrente de un restaurante.

_____ 11. Canadá está lejos de Europa.

_____ 12. El estado de Kansas está entre Colorado y Missouri.

_____ 13. Usualmente, un partido de béisbol es en un estadio.

_____ 14. Al lado de mi casa hay un jardín.

_____ 15. Las antenas encima de mi casa mejoran la recepción del televisor.

_____ 16. En la corte, los abogados están frente al juez (*judge*).

ejercicio   II-1-2

*In this exercise, you = second-person singular (**tú**).*

1. There is a book on top of the table. _____

2. John is to the right of me, and Felipe is to the left. _____

3. Do you live next door to our restaurant? _____

4. Every spring we plant (*sembrar*) flowers in front of the house. _____

_____

5. We need more light (*la iluminación*) above the paintings (*el cuadro*). _____

_____

6. People (*la gente*) across the country watch (*mirar*) the Olympics (*los juegos olímpicos*) on television.

_____

7. My favorite song is "Close to You." _____

8. Many people want to live far from the airport (*el aeropuerto*). _____

_____

9. Do you know that there is a tiger (*el tigre*) under your bed? _____

_____

10. Why are there so many (*tanto*) dogs outside your house? _____

_____

11. Who is in the kitchen with Dinah? _____

12. What do you have inside your mouth? _____

13. He works at the bank. _____

14. They are in the bank. _____

15. There isn't anything on (*the*) television tonight. _____

16. There is nothing between us. _____

17. Who is behind you? _____

18. The play (*la obra*) is in the theater. _____

Prepositions of Movement

In addition to telling where something or someone is, prepositions and prepositions that function as adverbs can reveal where something or someone is going.

examples:

Estas conchas **a lo largo de** la playa son hermosas.
These shells *along* the beach are beautiful.

Ayer, caminé **a lo largo de** la playa.
Yesterday, I walked *along* the beach.

The following prepositions all indicate movement:

along	**a lo largo de**
around	**alrededor de**
backward(s)	**hacia atrás**
beyond	**más allá de**
forward(s)	**hacia adelante**
sideways	**de lado**
through, throughout	**por**
toward	**hacia**

ejercicio   II-1-3

Underline the correct term in parentheses for each of the following sentences.

1. Es muy romántico caminar (a lo largo de / de lado) la playa.

2. No puedo ver (hacia adelante / más allá de) las estrellas.

3. Para hacer ejercicio todos los días, Jorge corre diez veces (hacia atrás / alrededor de) la pista (*track*).

4. El coche pasa (por / de lado) el túnel.

5. Para ir a Canadá, necesitas conducir (por / hacia) el norte.

6. Es necesario ir (hacia adelante / hacia atrás) en la autopista (*freeway*).

7. No quiero andar en bicicleta (a lo largo de / hacia adelante) la autopista. Es demasiado peligroso.

8. Si tú vas (hacia / alrededor de) el este, en dos o tres cuadras (*blocks*) vas a ver la tienda que buscas.

9. El ladrón (*robber*) buscó (alrededor de / por) la casa hasta encontrar el oro.

10. Los niños no deben ir (más allá de / de lado) este punto.

11. Cuando pones el coche en marcha atrás (*in reverse*), tú y el coche van (hacia adelante / hacia atrás).

12. En el juego "Sillas musicales", caminamos (más allá de / alrededor de) las sillas.

---

ejercicio   II-1-4

In this exercise, you = second-person singular (tú).

1. I run around the lake every morning. _____

2. Do you walk along the boulevard (*el bulevar*)? _____

3. The detective searches throughout the house. _____

4. He's always looking toward his goals (*la meta*). _____

5. Superman can fly (*volar*) through the air. _____

6. Every evening they walk through the mall (*el centro comercial*). _____

_____

7. If you look beyond that tree, you can see the roller coaster (*la montaña rusa*). _____

_____

8. Do you want to walk around the block (*la cuadra*) with me? _____

9. You can't go beyond the end (*el final*) of this block. _____

10. We can drive (*conducir*) toward the river and then walk along the path (*la senda*). _____

_____

11. Nancy Kerrigan can skate (*patinar*) forwards and backwards. _____

12. Superman can fly, but he doesn't fly backwards. _____

Prepositions of Geographical Location

The following prepositional phrases are the principal terms you will need to give and describe geographical directions. Note that in English, we often say "north of" instead of "to the north of." When using the Spanish expressions, keep in mind the complete phrase.

to the north of	**al norte de**
to the south of	**al sur de**
to the east of	**al este de**
to the west of	**al oeste de**
to the northeast of	**al nordeste (noreste) de**
to the northwest of	**al noroeste de**
to the southeast of	**al sudeste (sureste) de**
to the southwest of	**al sudoeste (suroeste) de**

examples:

Hay una gasolinera **al norte del** supermercado.
There's a gas station *north of* the supermarket.

La mina está **al nordeste del** bosque.
The mine is *to the northeast of* the forest.

ejercicio   II-1-5

Look at a map of the United States. Where are the following states in relation to Missouri? (The first question has been answered for you.)

1. ¿Dónde está Iowa?   <u>Iowa está al norte de Missouri.</u>_____

2. ¿Dónde está Arkansas? _____

3. ¿Dónde está Kansas?   _____

4. ¿Dónde está Illinois? _____

5. ¿Dónde está Michigan? _____

6. ¿Dónde está Nebraska? _____

7. ¿Dónde está Oklahoma? _____

8. ¿Dónde está Tennessee? _____

9. ¿Dónde está Louisiana? _____

10. ¿Dónde está Minnesota? _____

Prepositions of Origin and Destination

Prepositions are also used to express origin and destination. In reality, these prepositions are variations of prepositions that show direction. Think of these prepositions as revealing direction in time. Mentally, to reach the origin of something, you move toward the past; to reach the destination, you move toward the future.

Origin

because of, for	**a causa de, por**
by	**por, de** (*to indicate authorship*)
(all the way) from	**desde**
from	**de**
of	**de**

Destination

for (purpose/destination)	**para**
to	**a**
toward	**hacia**

examples:

Me encantan los poemas **de** Gabriela Mistral.
I love the poems *by* Gabriela Mistral. (*origin*)

Salen **para** Francia mañana.
They leave *for* France tomorrow. (*destination*)

ejercicio   II-1-6

Unless otherwise indicated, you = second-person singular.

1. Because of this cold (*el resfriado*), I can't go to the movies with my friends. _____

   _____

2. I'm reading a book by John Steinbeck. _____

3. This book is for you (*pl., formal*). _____

4. Greetings (*all the way*) from Cancún! _____

5. We're going to the mall (*el centro comercial*). Do you want to go with us? _____

   _____

6. These pearls (*la perla*) are from Japan. _____

7. All my friends from college (*la universidad*) are here. _____

   _____

8. What do they want from me? _____

9. I don't have anything for you. _____

10. He calls me (*all the way*) from Germany (*Alemania*) every week. _____

_____

11. Because of her attitude (*la actitud*) and bitterness (*la amargura*), she has no friends. _____

_____

12. The novel *Sophie's Choice* is by William Styron. _____

13. We are marching (*marchar*) to Pretoria. _____

14. One of them is going to win (*ganar*) the grand prize (*el premio gordo*)! _____

_____

15. I'm tired, and for this reason (*razón*) I'm going to take a nap (*dormir una siesta*). _____

_____

Prepositions of Time

Prepositions and prepositions that function as adverbs can be used to demonstrate a relationship in time. As with prepositions of location, the terms themselves do not change; only the function, or part of speech, changes.

To review, a term is a preposition when it connects two or more nouns and/or pronouns. In these cases, the verb almost always will be the linking verb *to be* (**ser** or **estar**). A term is an adverb when it modifies an action verb.

The following terms are used to express time.

after	**después de**
afterwards	**después**
before	**antes de**
beforehand	**antes**
during	**durante**
in	**por**
since	**desde**
to, until	**a**
until	**hasta**

examples:

Me esperarán **hasta** mañana.
They'll wait for me *until* tomorrow.

Llámame **antes de** las ocho.
Call me *before* eight.

Después de comer, no es bueno dormirse.
After eating, it's not good to fall asleep.

Tienes que preparar las verduras **antes.**
You must prepare the vegetables *beforehand.*

ejercicio   II-1-7

Underline the correct term in parentheses for each of the following sentences.

1. Comemos el postre (*dessert*) (antes de / después de) la comida.

2. Hay muchos anuncios (*commercials*) (durante / por) el programa de televisión.

3. La temporada (*season*) de béisbol es de abril (desde / hasta) octubre.

4. (Antes de / Por) un partido de béisbol, cantamos el himno nacional.

5. Juan ha vivido (*has lived*) en California (por / desde) 1981.

6. Muchas personas trabajan de lunes (a / durante) viernes.

7. Tenemos que lavar los platos (antes de / después de) la cena.

8. No es cortés hablar (antes de / durante) la película.

9. Es importante limpiar la casa (durante / antes de) la fiesta.

10. Muchos consultorios (*offices*) de dentista tocan música (hasta / durante) el día.

11. El senador está en una reunión, pero regresa a la oficina (antes / después).

12. Se pueden oír las noticias (por / hasta) las mañanas.

ejercicio   II-1-8

Unless otherwise indicated, you = second-person singular.

1. You don't have to be here until tomorrow. _____

2. I need to clean the garage before (*the*) winter. _____

3. A: It's cold, isn't it (¿*no?*)? B: Yes. Since Tuesday. _____

4. Some people believe that ghosts (*el fantasma*) live after death (*la muerte*). _____

_____

5. After (*the*) dinner, we always wash the dishes. _____

6. What do you want to do during our break (*el descanso*)? _____

7. What do you usually do in the afternoon? _____

8. What do you want to do before the dance (*el baile*)? _____

9. We usually talk during the commercials (*el anuncio*). _____

10. He's going to work here until March. _____

11. A: Don't you have milk? B: No. Not since Saturday. _____

12. They work from Monday to Friday. _____

13. We can watch the movie and go to the restaurant afterwards. _____

_____

14. I always chop (*picar*) the onions beforehand. _____

Prepositions of Location at the End of a Sentence or Clause

With many prepositional phrases that end in **de** (**encima de, cerca de, lejos de,** etc.), you only need to drop the **de** if you want the sentence or clause to end with the preposition, usually when the object of the preposition is understood.

El libro está **encima de** la mesa.   El libro está **encima.**
The book is *on top of* the table.   The book is *on top.*

With every rule there are exceptions. The following four terms must come at the end of a sentence or clause and cannot be followed by a noun. Usually, the object of the preposition is understood when these terms are used.

inside	**adentro**
downstairs, underneath	**abajo**
outside	**afuera**
upstairs, above	**arriba**

examples:

Estamos **adentro.**   Ellos están **afuera.**
We are *inside* (the house).   They are *outside* (the house).

ejercicio   II-1-9

Complete each sentence with one of the terms listed above.

1. El sótano está _____.

2. El desván (*attic*) está _____.

3. Los muebles elegantes están _____.

4. Los muebles del patio están _____.

5. En una casa grande, normalmente los dormitorios están _____.

6. Cuando hace mucho frío, pasamos el tiempo _____.

7. Jugamos al fútbol _____.

8. En muchas iglesias tradicionales, la sala social está _____.

9. Un gato sin garras (*claws*) debe quedarse (*remain*) _____.

10. No tenemos garaje, por eso estacionamos el coche _____.

ejercicio   II-1-10

*Answer the following questions using the prepositions **adentro, afuera, abajo, arriba.***

1. ¿Dónde está tu dormitorio? _____

2. ¿Dónde está tu coche o bicicleta ahora? _____

3. ¿Dónde estás tú ahora? _____

4. ¿Dónde duermen los murciélagos (*bats*) en una cueva? _____

5. ¿Dónde está el horno (*furnace*) de tu casa? _____

6. ¿Dónde estás durante un ciclón (*tornado*)? _____

7. ¿Dónde está el baño principal de tu casa? _____

8. ¿Dónde está el tejado (*roof*)? _____

9. ¿Dónde están los árboles más grandes? _____

10. ¿Dónde están los árboles decorados para la Navidad? _____

Para and Por

All students of Spanish discover quickly that the prepositions **para** and **por** are a force with which to be reckoned. At first, we discover that they both mean "for"; however, under closer inspection, we find out that each has several other meanings; some are shared by both, and others are unique to each one.

The issues encountered with **para** and **por** are sometimes compared with those of **ser** and **estar,** both of which translate as "to be." In the case of **ser** and **estar,** we have one (seemingly) clear-cut term in English and two terms in Spanish, each with a list of rules and baggage for us to absorb.

An important distinction between these two pairs of terms is that **ser** and **estar,** in most grammatical instances, are not interchangeable. What this means is that when a person makes an error using **ser** or **estar,** that error will register as a mistake in the mind of the listener (the bad news), but the listener nearly always will be able to "fix" the mistake in his or her mind and understand what the speaker intended (the good news).

Para and **por,** on the other hand, are grammatically interchangeable a good deal of the time. You can use one or the other, and you will produce a perfectly well-structured sentence (the good news). However, most listeners lack mind-reading skills, and they will therefore assume that you mean what you are actually saying, which is not always the case (the bad news).

Consider the following pair of sentences (their differences will be explained more clearly in other parts of the unit):

A. Luciano canta **para** Plácido.   B. Luciano canta **por** Plácido.

Both sentences translate as "Luciano sings *for* Plácido." But they have very different meanings. In this unit on **para** and **por,** you will see several ways in which English is ambiguous and Spanish is crystal clear.

In sentence A, Luciano is singing *to* Plácido: Luciano is on the stage, and Plácido is sitting happily in the audience listening to the music. In sentence B, Luciano is singing *on behalf of* Plácido: Plácido is nowhere to be found, and Luciano takes his place. In this context, Luciano is Plácido.

In a nutshell, think of **para** as an arrow; in one way or another, **para** tells us where something is going. **Por,** on the other hand, is like a balance scale, equalizing both sides of the preposition.

Thus, we must be extremely careful in using **para** and **por.** In this unit we will examine the various meanings of each one: first, **para;** then, **por.** Finally, we will mix them up, as we do in everyday conversation. **Para** and **por,** for all their tininess, provide the Spanish speaker with a rich source of describing various relationships of people and things.

Para

para =

A good image to have in mind when working with **para** is an arrow. Like an arrow, **para** goes ahead, away from its origin toward its destination, usually in a direct, straight route.

The uses of **para** can be cleanly placed into the following four categories: *destination, purpose, deadline,* and *standard.* With all four, which you will find in the more specific account below, the feeling is that of differentiating nouns in a sentence, of going ahead toward a specific goal or destination.

Para: Destination

Indicates real or figurative destination: **Para** indicates the destination of something or someone, whether that destination is real/physical or figurative/metaphorical. **Para** tells us where something is going, could go, or perhaps should go. In this context, **para** nearly always translates as "for."

Real/Physical:
Este jabón es **para** el baño.   Este teléfono es **para** esa oficina.
This soap is *for* the bathroom.   This telephone is *for* that office.

Figurative/Metaphorical:
Mi casa es buena **para** la fiesta.   Romeo es perfecto **para** Julieta.
My house is good *for* the party.   Romeo is perfect *for* Juliet.

Expresses the recipient of an action: **Para** tells us not only where, but also *to whom* something is going. The recipient always follows **para,** which translates as "for" in this context.

Tengo el dinero **para** Juan.   Estos regalos son **para** mí.
I have the money *for* John.   These gifts are *for* me.

Indicates direction and/or final travel destination: Often when we travel, there are stops along the way before our final destination. **Para** concerns itself only with the end of the road, so to speak. (See the section on **por** for dealing with the layovers.) When discussing your travels around the world or around your hometown, you will use **para** only to describe where you want to end up. In this context, **para** can mean either "to" or "for."

Los astronautas van **para** la luna.   Salimos **para** la iglesia a las nueve.
The astronauts go *to* the moon.   We leave *for* church at nine o'clock.

Indicates aim or objective of an action (+ profession):   **Para** is used to indicate the final destination of your studies, or what you want to be. In universities in the United States, we often talk about a major. In Spanish, a student majoring in biology could say, **"Estudio *para* médico,"**

which translates as "I'm studying *to be* a physician," or simply, "I'm studying medicine." The verb *to be* in this context is understood and therefore can be omitted. You can, if you want, include **ser: Estudio para *ser* médico.** Note that with this usage, the profession usually remains singular even when the subject is plural, as in the example on the right.

Ella estudia **para** electricista.
She is studying *to be* an electrician.

Ellos estudian **para** carpintero.
They are studying *to be* carpenters.

Para: Purpose

Expresses purpose (before an infinitive):   The reason a thing exists is its purpose. When describing what something does, or what it is for, we use **para** + the appropriate verb. Because a verb cannot be conjugated after a preposition, the format will always be **para** + *infinitive*. This use of **para** translates as "for."

Una pluma es **para** escribir.
A fountain pen is *for* writing.

Estos zapatos son **para** correr.
These shoes are *for* jogging.

Tells why one does something; "in order to" (before an infinitive):   When giving the reason for doing something, you use **para** + the appropriate infinitive. In this case, **para** means "to" or "in order to."

Yo como **para** vivir.
I eat *to* live.

Estudiamos **para** aprender.
We study *in order to* learn.

Para: Deadline

Expresses a specific time limit or deadline (in the future):   When you drop your clothing at the cleaners on Monday, you probably want them by Tuesday or definitely by the end of the week. You will use **para** to indicate that time limit or deadline. In this context, **para** translates usually as "by"; however, it can also mean "for," "on," or "before."

Necesito la ropa **para** el jueves.
I need the clothes *by* (*for, before*) Thursday.

Tenemos que hacer esto **para** esta noche.
We have to do this *by* tonight.

Expresses a limited timespan in the future: When describing an action that will stretch out over a specified period of time in the future, you use **para** to encompass this timespan. As a rule, this will be a generalized period of time, as opposed to a clock time of hours. This use of **para** translates as "for."

Él tiene empleo **para** el verano.
He has work *for* the summer.

Tenemos una casa reservada **para** dos semanas.
We have a house reserved *for* two weeks.

Para: Standard

Expresses a comparison to a certain standard: When something or someone goes outside the norm or beyond what is expected, and we make a comparison, we use **para** to draw attention to that distinction. **Para** in these cases translates as "for."

Paco es alto **para** su edad.
Paco is tall *for* his age.

Hace calor **para** enero.
It's warm *for* January.

Expresses an opinion or personal standard: In order to say, "in my opinion," you can say, literally, **"en mi opinión,"** or you can say more simply, **"para mí."** This construction works with names, as well as pronouns. In this context, **para** translates as "for."

Para mí, el español es hermoso.
In my opinion (For me), Spanish is beautiful.

Para Paco, Portland es la mejor ciudad.
In Paco's opinion (For Paco), Portland is the best city.

To summarize, the four categories of the uses of **para** are listed below. This list will be helpful in doing the exercises.

1. Destination
   a. Indicates real or figurative destination
   b. Expresses the recipient of an action
   c. Indicates direction and/or final travel destination
   d. Indicates aim or objective of an action (+ profession)
2. Purpose
   e. Expresses purpose (before an infinitive)
   f. Tells why one does something; "in order to" (before an infinitive)
3. Deadline
   g. Expresses a specific time limit or deadline (in the future)
   h. Expresses a limited timespan in the future
4. Standard
   i. Expresses a comparison to a certain standard
   j. Expresses an opinion or personal standard

ejercicio   II-2-1

*Write the letter from the preceding list that corresponds to the reason for using **para** in each of the following sentences.*

_____ 1. Tenemos que pagar los impuestos (*taxes*) para el 15 de abril.

_____ 2. Santa Claus sólo tiene carbón para ella.

_____ 3. Pongo la radio para escuchar la música.

_____ 4. Vamos para Amsterdam este verano.

_____ 5. Para Gregorio, un presidente debe ser diplomático.

_____ 6. Para recibir buenas notas (*grades*), necesitas trabajar mucho.

_____ 7. Camila toma clases para actriz.

_____ 8. Este jabón es para el cuerpo y ése es para la cara.

_____ 9. ¡Para un restaurante de cuatro estrellas, esta comida está horrible!

_____ 10. Este papel es para envolver regalos.

_____ 11. Para Ángela, mirar una película es una buena manera de pasar la noche.

_____ 12. Ellas estudian para bibliotecarias.

_____ 13. Está muy nublado para un día de junio.

_____ 14. Para mí, es muy bueno sacar fotos de ocasiones importantes.

_____ 15. Tienes que hacer algo para tu novia en el día de San Valentín.

_____ 16. Este detergente es para lavar la ropa.

_____ 17. Tengo empleo para el año que viene.

_____ 18. Salimos para la discoteca a la medianoche.

_____ 19. Este espejo (*mirror*) es para la entrada de la casa.

_____ 20. Ella es muy inteligente para una niña de sólo tres años.

ejercicio II-2-2

The words and expressions in bold type will translate as **"para."** *Unless otherwise indicated, you = second-person singular.*

1. This house is perfect **for** us. _____

2. We need a new table **for** the dining room. _____

3. **For** some people, it isn't important to have a car. _____

4. These shoes are **for** dancing the tango. _____

5. You have to read this book **by** Thursday. _____

6. He watches television **(in order) to** avoid (*evitar*) his problems. _____

   _____

7. I'm leaving **for** Africa tomorrow. _____

8. I'm studying **to be** a magician (*el mago*). _____

9. He's very polite (*cortés*) **for** a teenager (*el adolescente*). _____

   _____

10. Can you write the letter **by** Tuesday? _____

11. This food is **for** the cat. _____

12. **For** him, winter is wonderful, but **for** me, summer is the best season (*la estación*). _____

_____

13. She works a lot **in order to** get (*sacar*) good grades. _____

14. What time do you leave **for** work (*el trabajo*)? _____

15. These apples are not **for** eating. _____

Por

por =

Like a balance scale, **por** is the great equalizer. When dealing with **por,** you can often feel the balance on both sides of the term. We trade things because they are of perceived equal value. When we say how long something lasts, we are equating the action with an amount of time. When we substitute one thing or person for another, we consider the two items or persons of equal value, at least temporarily.

The uses of **por** can be cleanly placed into the following six categories: *duration, substitution, motivation, movement, emotions,* and *idioms.* With all six, which you will see in their variations below, the feeling is one of equating or combining nouns in a sentence, rather than differentiating them.

Por: Duration

Expresses duration of time: When expressing the duration of something—that is, telling how long something lasts—you use **por.** In this context, **por** translates as "for."

Cada día trabajamos **por** ocho horas.   Ellos van de vacaciones **por** dos semanas.
Every day we work *for* eight hours.   They go on vacation *for* two weeks.

Indicates periods of time during the 24-hour day: **Por** used before **la mañana, la tarde, la noche,** or **el día** indicates an unspecified amount of time, yet it implies that whatever is taking place lasts a while (as opposed to an extremely short time). In this context, **por** translates as "for," "at," "during," "on," or "throughout."

Tenemos clase **por** la noche.   Él toma café **por** el día.
We have class *at* night.   He drinks coffee *throughout* the day.

Ellos van al templo los viernes **por** la noche.   Voy al dentista el lunes **por** la tarde.
They go to synagogue *on* Friday nights.   I'm going to the dentist *on* Monday afternoon.

Expresses the English use of the Latin term *per:*   When we speak of times per day, minutes per hour, or the percentage of something, we use **por** to express this relationship. This use of **por** indicates duration or an amount of a whole.

Él lee tres libros **por** mes.   El diez **por ciento** no aprobó el examen.
He reads three books *per month.*   *Ten percent* didn't pass the exam.

Por: Substitution or Exchange

Indicates an equal exchange or trade: *Por* often implies an equality of the two things that it separates. Whenever we freely trade or purchase something, we do so because, at least to us, what we are giving is equal in value to what we are getting in return. In this context, **por** usually translates as "for."

Pagué cinco dólares **por** la pizza.
I paid five dollars *for* the pizza.

Juan cambió su manzana **por** una naranja.
Juan exchanged his apple *for* an orange.

Expresses substitution ("in/on behalf of," "in place of"):   Another use of **por** to indicate equality is any situation in which something or someone is being substituted for something or someone else. We see this in recipes, in the workplace, in the classroom, and at times when the original or principal ingredient or person is not available. In these sentences, **por** usually translates as "for," "in/on behalf of," or "in place of."

El vicepresidente habla **por** el presidente.
The vice-president speaks *on behalf of* the president.

Sustituyo margarina **por** mantequilla.
I substitute margarine *for* butter.

Expresses thanks and gratitude: When thanking someone for something that he or she has done for you or when expressing gratitude for a gift, you use **por**. This is another example of **por** as an equalizer. This is why we say that we give thanks *for* a kind deed: the thanks balance the act of giving. For this use, **por** usually translates as "for."

Gracias **por** las flores.
Thank you *for* the flowers.

Te doy las gracias **por** tu ayuda.
I thank you *for* your help.

Por: Motivation

Indicates having done something or "because of" (*por* + infinitive):   **Por** placed before an infinitive generally translates as "because of" or "due to," and it leads the speaker to reveal his or her motive for or reason behind something. The verb that follows must be in the infinitive. In English, this verb translates as a gerund, which means that it actually is a verb in a noun's clothing, and it always ends in *-ing*.

Por ganar la lotería, ellos son ricos.
Due to winning the lottery, they are rich.

Él no trabaja hoy **por estar** enfermo.
He's not working today *because of his being* sick.

Expresses a motive for doing something: **Por** in this context tells why a person does something because of a specific motive and can translate as "for" or "because of."

Vamos a la tienda **por** mantequilla.
We're going to the store *for* butter.

Reconstruimos la casa **por** la tormenta.
We're rebuilding the house *because of* the storm.

Tells why something or someone is a certain way (*por* + noun or infinitive):   **Por** can be used to tell why something is the way it is due to or because of another event. It expresses the motive or reason behind a state of being. In these sentences, **por** often precedes a noun. In this context, **por** can translate as "for," or "due to," or "because of."

Soy más fuerte **por la experiencia.**
I am stronger *because of the experience.*

Beethoven es famoso **por su música.**
Beethoven is famous *for his music.*

Soy más fuerte **por tener la experiencia.**
I am stronger *for having the experience.*

Beethoven es famoso **por componer su música.**
Beethoven is famous *for composing his music.*

Paco es popular **por su personalidad.**
Paco is popular *because of his personality.*

Ella ahorra mucho dinero **por los cupones.**
She saves a lot of money *due to coupons.*

Paco es popular **por ser tan inteligente.**
Paco is popular *for being so intelligent.*

Ella ahorra mucho dinero **por usar cupones.**
She saves a lot of money *due to using coupons.*

Por: Movement

Expresses means of transportation: When you want to tell how you are getting somewhere, you will use **por** before whatever mode of transportation you plan to use. Below are listed some common forms of transportation. This use of **por** translates as "by" or "on."

por autobús	by bus	**por ferrocarril, tren**	by rail, train
por avión	by airplane	**por coche (carro)**	by car

Note: The preposition **en** is also used in this way: **en avión, en tren,** etc.

Martín va al trabajo **por autobús.**
Martin goes to work *on the bus.*

Viajan de Londres a París **por tren.**
They travel from London to Paris *by train.*

Expresses means of sending messages or information: To talk about sending a message, you almost certainly will use the preposition **por.** In this context, por can translate as "by," "on," or "via."

por computadora	by computer	**por e-mail**	by e-mail
por correo	by mail	**por fax**	by fax
por correo electrónico	by e-mail	**por teléfono**	by phone; on the telephone

Le envío un regalo **por correo.**
I'm sending him a gift *by mail.*

No es bueno discutir **por teléfono.**
It's not good to fight *on the telephone.*

Indicates the point of a temporary stop: If you are stopping by someone's house or a store, or if you have a layover in a certain city, and if none of these destinations is your final one, this temporary stop can be indicated by using **por.** (Contrast this with the use of **para** to indicate final destination.) In this context, **por** translates as "by" or "through."

Voy **por** el banco antes de ir al teatro.
I'm going *by* the bank before going to the theater.

Pasamos **por** Detroit en el viaje a París.
We're going *through* Detroit on the trip to Paris.

Indicates movement in an area: While **para** indicates movement to or toward a destination, **por** implies that the person already is there and is moving around in a general, nonspecific direction. In such sentences, **por** can mean "around," "through," "throughout," or "by."

Nos paseamos **por** el parque.
We stroll *around* (*through*) the park.

El detective busca **por** la casa.
The detective searches *throughout* the house.

Por: Emotions

Expresses a liking (or disliking) or an emotion for someone or something: When you have something tangible, such as a book, for someone, you will use **para.** However, when what you have or feel for somone is intangible, such as respect, you use **por.**

Think of it like this: when you give something tangible away, you are left with nothing; your hand is empty. But you cannot give away emotions; you can only move them around. No matter how much love you give to someone, you still will be filled with love. In fact, the more of an emotion that you give, the more you retain. In this context, **por** nearly always translates as "for."

Juan tiene mucho amor **por** su esposa.
John has a lot of love *for* his wife.

Tengo respeto **por** mis amigos.
I have respect *for* my friends.

Por: Idioms

Appears in idiomatic expressions: **Por** is used in hundreds of idiomatic expressions. If you look in a dictionary of Spanish idiomatic usage, you will find several pages of phrases that begin with **por.** The following list contains some of the more commonly used expressions.

por allí	around there; that way
por aquí	around here; this way
por ejemplo	for example
por eso (esto)	therefore
por favor	as a favor; please
por fin	at last; finally
por (lo) general	as a rule; generally
por medio de	by means of
por lo menos	at least
por primera vez	for the first time
por separado	separately
por supuesto	of course
por todas partes	everywhere
por todos lados	all over; everywhere; on all sides

To summarize, the six categories of the uses of **por** are listed below. This list will be helpful in doing the exercises.

1. Duration
   a. Expresses duration of time
   b. Indicates periods of time during the 24-hour day
   c. Expresses use of the Latin term *per*
2. Substitution or Exchange
   d. Indicates an equal exchange or trade
   e. Expresses substitution ("in behalf of," "in place of")
   f. Expresses thanks and gratitude
3. Motivation
   g. Indicates having done something or "because of" (*por* + infinitive)
   h. Expresses a motive for doing something
   i. Tells why something or someone is a certain way (*por* + noun or infinitive)
4. Movement
   j. Expresses means of transportation
   k. Expresses means of sending messages or information
   l. Indicates the point of a temporary stop
   m. Indicates movement in an area
5. Emotions
   n. Expresses a liking (or disliking) or an emotion for someone or something
6. Idioms
   o. Appears in idiomatic expressions

ejercicio   II-2-3

*Write the letter from the preceding list that corresponds to the reason for using **por** in each of the following sentences.*

_____ 1. Ella corre por media hora cada día.

_____ 2. Vamos a Amsterdam por avión.

_____ 3. Caminamos por el centro comercial, pero no compramos nada.

_____ 4. Pagamos cien dólares por la silla.

_____ 5. El coche va a sesenta millas por hora.

_____ 6. La policía buscó por todas partes sin encontrar al ladrón (*thief*).

_____ 7. No tengo ningún sentimiento por ti.

_____ 8. Ella siempre duerme una siesta por la tarde.

_____ 9. Gracias por las manzanas.

_____ 10. Él siempre recibe una *A* por estudiar mucho.

_____ 11. Tengo laringitis. Tienes que hablar por mí.

_____ 12. Voy por tu casa antes de ir al cine.

_____ 13. La casa fue destruida por el terremoto.

_____ 14. Voy al centro comercial por un vestido.

_____ 15. Vamos al teatro el sábado por la noche.

_____ 16. No quiero pagar más de diez dólares por una libra de café.

_____ 17. Ellos siempre compran la comida por separado.

_____ 18. Manejamos por la ciudad en busca del restaurante perfecto.

_____ 19. Puedes enviarme la información por correo electrónico.

_____ 20. Nadie trabaja por mí cuando estoy enfermo.

_____ 21. ¿Cuál es la razón por la que envías estas flores?

_____ 22. Ellos prefieren viajar por ferrocarril.

_____ 23. Montaigne es conocido por sus ensayos (*essays*).

_____ 24. Te doy muchas gracias por tu bondad (*kindness*).

_____ 25. Por comprar tantas cosas, ella está sin plata (*broke*).

ejercicio   II-2-4

Translate the following sentences. The word or phrase to be replaced by **por** *(or* **por** *+ idiom) is in bold type. Unless otherwise indicated, you = second-person singular.*

1. We go to school **by** bus. _____

2. You can have those shoes **for** ten dollars. _____

3. He has **at least** twenty cats. _____

4. When I travel, I always walk **through** the city and I investigate (*investigar*) everything. _____
   _____

5. We read the newspaper **for** thirty minutes every morning. _____

6. Juanita is sick today. Can you work **for** her? _____

7. I'm going to the supermarket **for** milk, butter, and eggs. _____

8. Every **Monday night** he watches football (*el fútbol americano*) on television. _____
   _____

9. **Because of** her allergies (*las alergias*), she can't touch the cat. _____

10. Thanks **for** nothing. _____

11. **For** giving so much (*tanto*) to others, she deserves (*merecer*) a medal (*la medalla*). _____
    _____

12. Ninety **percent** of all the dentists say that this toothpaste (*la pasta de dientes*) is horrible. _____
    _____

13. He comes **by** my house now and then (*de vez en cuando*). _____
    _____

14. I only have admiration (*la estimación*) **for** you. _____

15. I now understand the differences between *por* and *para* **for** the first time. _____
    _____

16. You can send me the contracts (*el contrato*) **by** fax. _____

ejercicio   II-2-5

*Fill in the blank with the appropriate use of **para** or **por**. Then give the reason for your choice.*

1. Tengo algunas cosas _____ ti. _____

2. Juan es muy humilde (*modest*) _____ un hombre tan inteligente y rico. _____

_____

3. Gracias _____ los mapas. Puedo usarlos en mi viaje a España. _____

_____

5. Cuando visito un museo, siempre camino _____ todas las galerías. _____

_____

6. El concierto comienza a las ocho. Quiero llegar al teatro _____ las siete y media. _____

_____

7. Los juguetes de Mattel son _____ niños. _____

8. Yo tomo café _____ la mañana y _____ la tarde, pero nunca _____ la noche.

_____

9. Estas toallas (*towels*) son _____ el baño principal. _____

_____

10. Batman y Robin siempre viajan _____ Batmobile, y nunca _____ autobús.

_____

11. Este restaurante es demasiado costoso. ¡Veinte dólares _____ una ensalada es ridículo!

_____

12. ¿Estás listo (*ready*)? Salimos _____ la biblioteca ahora. _____

_____

13. Tengo hambre. ¿Hay un restaurante _____ aquí? _____

_____

14. No hay clases hoy y nada está abierto _____ la nieve. _____

_____

15. Me abono (*subscribe*) a dos periódicos _____ saber las noticias del mundo. _____

16. Cuando la actriz principal está enferma, su suplente (*understudy*) se presenta _____ ella.

17. Me cepillo los dientes más o menos cinco veces _____ día. _____

18. El dentista cree que debemos cepillarnos los dientes _____ lo menos dos veces al día.

19. Martín cree que el sistema métrico es el mejor, pero _____ mí, prefiero pies y pulgadas.

20. Antes de la fiesta, vamos _____ la tienda a comprar unos refrescos. _____

21. Siento nada menos que (*nothing but*) disgusto _____ ellos. _____

22. Uso e-mail _____ escribir notas a mis colegas. _____

23. No tenemos ni luces ni electricidad _____ no pagar la cuenta de utilidades a tiempo.

24. John Phillips Sousa es famoso _____ sus marchas. _____

25. Cada día hablo con mi esposo _____ teléfono. _____

26. Después de veinte años, _____ fin Carlota ganó la lotería. _____

27. Comemos _____ vivir. _____

28. Vamos a tener una fiesta el sábado _____ la noche. _____

29. Solamente el treinta _____ ciento de los médicos recomiendan esta medicina. _____

_____

30. Ustedes tienen que terminar el proyecto _____ finales del mes. _____

_____

ejercicio   II-2-6

*The following eight pairs of sentences differ either very little or not at all, except in the use of **para** or **por**. First, translate each sentence and then describe its meaning based on the use of **para** or **por**.*

   example:

   A. Juan cocina para Juanita.
   B. Juan cocina por Juanita.

   answer:

   A. Juan cooks for Juanita. Destination: Juanita is in the dining room, awaiting her meal.
   B. Juan cooks for Juanita. Substitution: Juanita should cook the meal, but Juan is doing it for her.

1. A. Puedes tener mi camisa para tu falda.

_____

_____

   B. Puedes tener mi camisa por tu falda.

_____

_____

2. A. Vamos para su casa esta noche.

_____

_____

   B. Vamos por su casa esta noche.

_____

_____

3. A. Tengo muchas muestras (*samples*) de champú y jabón para el viaje.

_____

_____

B. Tengo muchas muestras de champú y jabón por el viaje.

_____

_____

4. A. Martín y Dorotea tienen muchos juguetes para Daisy.

_____

_____

B. Martín y Dorotea tienen mucho amor por Daisy.

_____

_____

5. A. Judith baila para Twyla.

_____

_____

B. Judith baila por Twyla.

_____

_____

6. A. Conducimos para el parque.

_____

_____

B. Conducimos por el parque.

_____

_____

7. A. Estas cremas son para las alergias.

_____

_____

B. Estas alergias son por las cremas.

_____

_____

8. A. Para mí, esta sopa está mala.

_____

_____

B. Por mí, esta sopa está mala.

_____

_____

traducción   II-2-7

This is a story for everyone. There is a woman who lives in Texas. She works for a large company, but she works for very little money. She needs more money for food and clothing. Every Friday afternoon, when she buys gasoline, she pays two dollars extra for lottery tickets. She chooses the lottery numbers for (*because of*) ages of friends and for special dates. This week, for the first time, she wins. She wins a billion dollars. It is enough money (*in order*) to buy everything that she wants. First she buys gifts for all her friends. Of course, they tell her, "Thank you for these gifts." Normally, she doesn't pay more than fifty dollars for a dress; however, for winning the lottery, tomorrow she is going to Paris in order to buy a dress for fifty thousand dollars. Are you happy for her?

vocabulario

age	**la edad**	gasoline	**la gasolina**
billion	**mil millones**	however	**sin embargo**
(to) choose	**escoger**	lottery	**la lotería**
company	**la compañía**	number	**el número**
date	**la fecha**	story	**la historia**
enough	**suficiente**	ticket	**el billete**
extra	**adicional**	(to) win	**ganar**

_____

_____

_____

_____

_____

_____

_____

Verbs and Prepositions

The relationship between verbs and prepositions is a special one. In some cases, the preposition exists in the definition of the verb itself; in other cases, the meaning of the verb depends upon the preposition that follows it. In this unit, you will expand your vocabulary by exploring the intricate relationship between verbs and prepositions.

Verbs Whose Meanings Include a Preposition

There are many Spanish verbs whose definitions in English include a preposition. It is important to know these verbs in order to resist the temptation to add a preposition when none is needed or when adding one is grammatically incorrect. A list of the more common verbs is provided below for you. In all cases the understood, or contained, word is italicized in the definition.

examples:

Busco mis zapatos.
I'm looking for my shoes.

Miras las pinturas.
You look at the paintings.

El plato **huyó** con la cuchara.
The dish *ran away* with the spoon.

Los trapos **empapan** el aceite.
The rags *soak up* the oil.

El jardinero **arranca** la maleza.
The gardener *pulls out* the weeds.

Escuchamos música.
We listen to music.

Encendemos las luces.
We turn on the lights.

Apagamos las luces.
We turn off (out) the lights.

The following are commonly used Spanish verbs whose definitions in English include a preposition. Note that the definitions given here are not complete for every verb; some have additional definitions that do not include a preposition in English.

agradecer	to be grateful (thankful) *for*
anhelar	to yearn (long) *to*
apagar	to turn *off*
aprobar (o→ue)	to approve *of*
arrancar	to root *up;* to pull *out;* to turn *on* (car)
atravesar (e→ie)	to go (run) *through;* to go *across*

139

averiguar	to find *out*
bajar	to go *down;* to descend
borrar	to cross *out;* to erase
botar	to throw *away;* to toss *out*
buscar	to look *for*
caer(se)	to fall *down*
calentar (e→ie)	to heat (warm) *up*
colgar (o→ue)	to hang *up*
conocer	to be acquainted *with;* to know (a person or place)
cortar	to cut *off;* to cut *out*
criar	to bring *up;* to rear
derribar	to knock *down;* to tear *down;* to overthrow
destacar	to stand *out*
elegir	to elect (choose) *to*
empapar	to absorb; to soak (sponge) *up*
encender (e→ie)	to turn *on* (lights)
enseñar	to point *out;* to teach
entregar	to hand *over;* to deliver
envolver (o→ue)	to wrap *up*
escuchar	to listen *to*
esperar	to wait *for;* to hope *for*
huir	to run away, flee *from*
ignorar	to be ignorant (unaware) *of*
indicar	to point *out*
llevar	to carry (take) *away*
lograr	to succeed *in;* to manage *to*
merecer	to deserve *to*
mirar	to look *at*
organizar	to set *up;* to organize
pagar	to pay *for*
pedir (e→i)	to ask *for*
pisar	to step *on;* to trample
platicar	to talk *over,* discuss
poder	to be able *to*
poner	to turn *on* (an appliance)
preferir	to prefer *to*
pretender	to seek (aspire) *to;* to claim *to*
quitar	to take *off*
recoger	to pick *up*
rogar (o→ue)	to beg *for;* to pray *for*
saber	to know how *to* (do something)
sacar	to take *out*
salir	to go *out* (of a place, on a date), leave
señalar	to point *out,* show
separar	to set *apart;* to separate
soler (o→ue)	(*soler* + infinitive) to be accustomed *to;* to be in the habit *of*
soplar	to blow *out*
subir	to go *up;* to come *up;* to get *on* (a train, bus, etc.)
tachar	to cross *out;* to erase; to correct
tender (e→ie)	to hang *out* (laundry); to spread *out*
yacer	to lie *down*

¿Verdadero o falso?

_____ 1. Usualmente, yo como en un restaurante, pero a veces llevo la comida.

_____ 2. Antes de preparar la carne, siempre quito la grasa (*fat*).

_____ 3. Vanna White señala las letras en el popular programa "La rueda de la fortuna".

_____ 4. Todos los días salgo antes de las ocho de la mañana.

_____ 5. El trabajo del detective con frecuencia es averiguar quién es el asesino (*murderer*).

_____ 6. El gallo atraviesa la calle para llegar al otro lado.

_____ 7. Me encanta soplar las velitas (*candles*) en la torta (*cake*) de cumpleaños.

_____ 8. Siempre pago mi ropa con cheque.

_____ 9. Yo sé bailar el merengue.

_____ 10. Yo merezco ganar la lotería.

_____ 11. Cuelgo el teléfono cuando me llama un vendedor a quien no conozco.

_____ 12. Las personas que vuelan en primera clase suben antes que los pasajeros en la clase turista.

_____ 13. Siempre pongo la radio cuando conduzco (*drive*) largas distancias.

_____ 14. Yo suelo estudiar por la noche y trabajar por el día.

_____ 15. ¡Quiero huir corriendo de mi casa ahora!

_____ 16. Mozart destaca por su música.

ejercicio   II-3-1

Consult the list of verbs as you translate the following sentences.

1. I am grateful for everything. _____

2. A: What are you looking for? B: I'm looking for my glasses (*los anteojos*). _____

_____

3. Where should we hang up our coats (*el abrigo*)? _____

4. I like to listen to classical music (*la música clásica*). _____

_____

5. You can pay for the clothing in cash (*en efectivo*) or with a credit card (*la tarjeta de crédito*). _____

_____

6. The babysitter (*la niñera*) picks up the toys (*el juguete*). _____

7. He crosses out all his mistakes (*el error*). _____

8. Tonight Carlota is going to go out with Guillermo. She is very excited (*ilusionado*). _____

_____

9. I always take out the garbage (*la basura*). You should take out the garbage once in a while (*de vez en cuando*). _____

_____

10. The lawyer hands over the evidence (*la evidencia*) to the judge (*el juez*). _____

_____

11. The rags (*el trapo*) soak up the oil (*el aceite*). _____

12. The mail carrier (*el cartero*) always steps on my roses. _____

13. I need more money. I'm going to ask for a raise (*el aumento*) tomorrow. _____

_____

14. How long (*¿Por cuánto tiempo*) do we have to wait for the bus? _____

_____

15. You can turn on the lights here and turn off the lights over there (*allá*). _____

_____

Verbs That Follow Prepositions

When a verb directly follows a preposition, there is only one rule to remember:

The verb following a preposition remains in the infinitive.

There is no exception to this rule. Usually the English translation of the infinitive will be in the gerund, or *-ing* form; however, at times the verb may translate as the infinitive as well.

Antes de comer, me lavo las manos.
Before eating, I wash my hands.

Después de comer, lavo los platos.
After eating, I wash the dishes.

En vez de estudiar, voy a dormir.
Instead of studying, I'm going to sleep.

Para recibir una *A*, necesitas trabajar duro.
In order to receive an *A*, you need to work hard.

Además de andar, puedo masticar chicle.
In addition to walking, I can chew gum.

Pienso **en conseguir** un gato.
I am thinking *of getting* a cat.

¿Verdadero o falso?

_____ 1. Además de tocar la guitarra, Bruce Springsteen también canta.

_____ 2. Antes de comprar un libro, normalmente leo uno o dos capítulos en la librería.

_____ 3. A veces, en vez de cepillarme los dientes, mastico chicle.

_____ 4. Después de ganar las elecciones, el nuevo presidente cumple (*keeps*) las promesas.

_____ 5. Además de tomar esta clase de español, tomo por lo menos (*at least*) dos clases adicionales.

_____ 6. Para mantener un coche, se necesita cambiar el aceite cada tres meses.

_____ 7. Después de ganar la Serie Mundial, los jugadores van directamente a Disneyworld.

_____ 8. Pienso en comprar un coche nuevo.

_____ 9. Normalmente me ducho antes de acostarme.

_____ 10. Pienso en renunciar a (*quitting*) mi trabajo.

_____ 11. Para estar a la moda, es necesario gastar (*spend*) muchísimo dinero por la ropa.

_____ 12. Este año, en lugar de cortar (*mow*) el césped (*lawn*), voy a comprar una cabra (*goat*).

ejercicio   II-3-2

1. We're going to drive to Vermont instead of flying. _____

2. Before buying the eggs, you should look inside the carton (*el cartón*). _____

_____

3. I always feel better after exercising (*hacer ejercicio*). _____

4. Besides being able to fly, Superman can see through (*a través de*) walls (*la pared*). _____

_____

5. I'm thinking about writing a novel. _____

6. In order to get (*llegar*) to the bank, you should turn (*doblar*) right on Park Avenue. _____

_____

7. Do you want to swim instead of playing golf? _____

8. She always eats ten tacos after swimming. _____

9. What do you have to do before leaving? _____

10. I'm going to a lecture (*la conferencia*) about using computers. _____

_____

11. In addition to boiling (*hervir*) water, this stove (*la estufa*) can boil milk! _____

_____

12. John has to take three more (*otras tres*) classes in order to graduate (*graduarse*). _____

_____

Verbs that Require a Preposition

Many Spanish verbs require the use of a preposition before the subsequent word, whether it is a noun or another verb (in its infinitive form). There is some method to this, and this is discussed in each of the following six sections. However, for the most part, these verbs, along with their respective prepositions, must be learned just as one learns other vocabulary terms.

Listed below are several verbs that require prepositions when preceding another word. These verbs are arranged alphabetically and are grouped according to the preposition each one takes. Following each verb is the most common part or parts of speech the verb will precede, then its English equivalent, and finally the result of the clause created, such as **cuidar a** (*n.*), to take care of (someone). Using this information, you could write: **Yo *cuido a* Juan** (I take care of Juan). Or the entry, **acabar de** (*v.*), to have just (done something), gives you enough information to write: **María *acaba de* escribir una carta** (María has just written a letter).

Important: In the entries below, when a verb takes **a**, note that this **a** is an actual preposition. Be careful not to confuse the preposition **a** with the personal **a,** which is placed after all verbs when the stated direct object is a person.

The abbreviations in the lists in this unit are as follows:

(*v.*) verb
(*n.*) noun

a

Verbs that are followed by **a** often are referred to as "springboard verbs" because they mark the beginning of an action. As you look through the following list of verbs, you will find that many of them move toward an action or lead a person ahead, either literally or figuratively.

Remember that the preposition **a** means "to," and that when you go to something, you are moving ahead, going forward.

acertar a (*v.*)	to manage to, succeed in (doing something)
acostumbrarse a (*n., v.*)	to become used to (someone, something, doing something)
adaptarse a (*n., v.*)	to adapt oneself to (something, a situation, doing something)
adelantarse a (*n., v.*)	to step forward to (someone, something, doing something)
animar a (*v.*)	to encourage to (do something)

animarse a *(v.)*	to decide, make up one's mind to (do something)
aprender a *(v.)*	to learn to (do something)
apresurarse a *(n., v.)*	to hasten to, hurry to (somewhere, do something)
arriesgarse a *(v.)*	to risk (doing something)
asistir a *(n.)*	to attend (something, a function)
asomarse a *(n.)*	to appear at, look out from (something)
aspirar a *(n., v.)*	to aspire to (be something, someone, do something)
atreverse a *(v.)*	to dare to (do something)
aventurarse a *(v.)*	to venture to (do something)
ayudar a *(v.)*	to help to (do something), to aid in (doing something)
burlar a *(n.)*	to deceive, play a trick on (someone)
comenzar a *(v.)*	to begin to (do something)
comprometerse a *(v.)*	to make a commitment to (do something)
condenar a *(v.)*	to condemn to (do something)
consagrarse a *(n.)*	to devote oneself to (someone, something)
contribuir a *(n., v.)*	to contribute to (something, doing something)
convidar a *(n., v.)*	to invite to (a function, do something)
correr a *(n., v.)*	to run to (somewhere, do something)
cuidar a *(n.)*	to care for, take care of (a person)
dar a *(n.)*	to face (something)
dar cuerda a *(n.)*	to wind (a watch)
decidirse a *(v.)*	to decide to (do something)
dirigirse a *(n., v.)*	to go to (a place); to address (someone); to direct oneself to (doing something)
disponerse a *(v.)*	to prepare to, be disposed to (do something)
empezar a *(v.)*	to begin to (do something)
enseñar a *(v.)*	to teach to (do something)
forzar a *(v.)*	to force to (do something)
impulsar a *(v.)*	to impel to (do something)
incitar a *(v.)*	to incite to (do something)
inducir a *(v.)*	to induce to (do something)
inspirar a *(v.)*	to inspire to (do something)
instar a *(v.)*	to urge to (do something)
invitar a *(n., v.)*	to invite to (a function, something, do something)
ir a *(n., v.)*	to go to (a place); to be going to (do something)
limitarse a *(v.)*	to limit oneself to (do something)
llegar a *(n., v.)*	to arrive at (a place); to be going to (do something)
meterse a *(v.)*	to take up (doing something)
montar a *(n.)*	to ride (something—a horse)
negarse a *(v.)*	to refuse to (do something)
obligar a *(v.)*	to oblige to (do something)
ofrecerse a *(v.)*	to offer to, promise to, volunteer to (do something)
oler a *(n.)*	to smell like (something)
oponerse a *(n., v.)*	to oppose, be in opposition to (something, doing something)
pararse a *(v.)*	to stop (to do something)
parecerse a *(n.)*	to resemble (someone, something) physically
pasar a *(n., v.)*	to pass to, proceed to (something, doing something)
persuadir a *(v.)*	to persuade to (do something)
ponerse a *(v.)*	to begin to, set out to (do something)
prestarse a *(v.)*	to lend oneself to (doing something)

probar a *(v.)*	to try to, attempt to (do something)
quedarse a *(v.)*	to stay to, remain to (do something)
rebajarse a *(n., v.)*	to stoop to (someone, a situation, doing something)
reducirse a *(n., v.)*	to reduce (a situation or oneself) to (something, do something)
rehusar a *(v.)*	to refuse to (do something)
renunciar a *(n.)*	to renounce, give up, quit (something, a job)
resignarse a *(n., v.)*	to resign oneself to (something, doing something)
resistirse a *(n., v.)*	to resist (something, doing something)
resolverse a *(v.)*	to make up one's mind to, resolve to (do something)
retirarse a *(n., v.)*	to retire to (a place, do something)
romper a *(v.)*	to start suddenly to (do something)
saber a *(n.)*	to taste like (something)
sentarse a *(n., v.)*	to sit down to (something, do something)
someterse a *(n., v.)*	to submit oneself to (something, doing something)
sonar a *(n.)*	to sound like (something)
subir a *(n.)*	to go up to, climb, get on (something)
venir a *(n., v.)*	to come to (a place, do something)
volver a *(n., v.)*	to return to (a place); to (do something) again

¿Verdadero o falso?

_____ 1. Doy cuerda a mi reloj cada día.

_____ 2. Me niego a volar cuando está lloviendo.

_____ 3. Yo creo que el pavo sabe a pollo.

_____ 4. Nadie puede forzarme a hacer nada.

_____ 5. Siempre rompo a llorar en una boda.

_____ 6. Quiero renunciar a mi trabajo.

_____ 7. Después de sentarme a comer, rehúso a contestar el teléfono.

_____ 8. Nunca me rebajo a robar dulces de un niño.

_____ 9. Nadie puede persuadirme a comer una carpa dorada (*goldfish*), ni por un millón de dólares.

_____ 10. Me parezco a uno de mis primos.

_____ 11. Peter Jennings se parece a James Bond.

_____ 12. A veces el ronroneo (*purring*) de un gato suena a un barco de motor.

_____ 13. La memoria de la madre Teresa me inspira a ser una mejor persona.

_____ 14. Mi casa da al este.

_____ 15. Cuando subo a mi coche, me pongo el cinturón de seguridad inmediatamente.

ejercicio   II-3-3

*You may consult the list of verbs that require **a** as you translate these sentences.*

1. This sounds like a lie. _____

2. She bursts out crying (*llorar*) every time that she remembers the pain (*el dolor*) of her childhood

   (*la niñez*). _____

3. He's going to quit his job because his company (*la compañía*) is going to begin to downsize (*recortar*

   al personal). _____

4. Sooner or later (*tarde o temprano*) you have to resign yourself to the fact (*el hecho de*) that some

   people are not honest (*honrado*). _____

5. You can't obligate/force us to do anything that we don't want to do. _____

   _____

6. Benjamín winds his watch every day at nine o'clock in the morning. _____

   _____

7. Mrs. Goncalvo encourages her children to study the fine arts (*las bellas artes*). _____

   _____

8. In this house we sit down to eat dinner (*cenar*) at seven o'clock sharp (*en punto*). _____

   _____

9. What time do we get on the train? _____

10. It's impossible to force Carmen to get on the roller coaster (*la montaña rusa*). _____

    _____

11. Mateo says that snake meat (*la carne de culebra*) tastes like chicken. _____

    _____

12. Oscar Wilde says that he can resist everything but (*salvo*) temptation (*la tentación*). _____

    _____

13. In this section of the book, we learn how to use verbs that take (*tomar*) the preposition *a*. _____

    _____

14. Some athletes (*el atleta*) become used to receiving and spending (*gastar*) lots of money. _____

_____

15. Richard is not disposed to giving us anything today. He is not in the mood (*de humor*). _____

_____

con

Verbs that require the preposition **con** sometimes clearly have the meaning "with," as in **asociarse con,** which means "to associate with." At other times we must unscramble the real meaning of the verb to understand more clearly why it takes **con.**

For example, the verb **casarse con,** which means "to marry," has as its root the noun **la casa** (house). The verb **casarse con** actually means "to set up a house for oneself with (someone)." Another commonly used verb, **encontrarse con** (to run into, meet up with), means literally, "to find oneself with."

aburrirse con (*n.*)	to be or get bored with (someone, something)
acabar con (*n.*)	to finish with/off, get rid of (something, someone)
amenazar con (*n., v.*)	to threaten with (something, doing something)
asociarse con (*n.*)	to associate with, team up with (someone)
asustarse con (*n.*)	to be afraid of, be frightened by (someone, something)
bastar con (*n., v.*)	(3rd-person) to be sufficient, have enough of (something, doing something)
casarse con (*n.*)	to marry (someone)
comerciar con (*n.*)	to trade in/with (a person, a business)
conformarse con (*n., v.*)	conform to, resign oneself to, make do (something, doing something)
contar con (*n.*)	to count on (someone, something)
contentarse con (*n.*)	to content oneself with (something)
dar con (*n.*)	to come upon (someone, something)
disfrutar con (*n.*)	to enjoy (someone, something)
divertirse con (*n.*)	to enjoy, have fun/a good time with (someone, something)
encontrarse con (*n.*)	to meet up with, run into (someone)
enfadarse con (*n.*)	to get angry at/with (someone, something)
enojarse con (*n.*)	to get angry at/with (someone, something)
equivocarse con (*n.*)	to make a mistake about, be mistaken about (someone, something)
espantarse con (*n.*)	to become afraid of (someone, something)
juntarse con (*n.*)	to associate with, join (forces) with (someone)
limpiar con (*n.*)	to clean (something) with (something)
llenar con (*n.*)	to fill (something) with (something)
meterse con (*n.*)	to bother, pick a fight with (someone, something)
preocuparse con (*n.*)	to worry about (someone, something)
recrearse con (*n.*)	to amuse oneself with (something)
romper con (*n.*)	to break up with, break off relations with (someone)
salir con (*n.*)	to go out with, date (someone)
soñar con (*n., v.*)	to dream of/about (someone, something, doing something)
tratar(se) con (*n.*)	to associate with, have dealings with (someone, something)
tropezarse con (*n.*)	to bump into (something, someone), stumble over (something)

¿Verdadero o falso?

_____ 1. A veces me encuentro con mis amigos para tomar un café.

_____ 2. Disfruto mucho con los discos de Gloria Estefan.

_____ 3. Un día quiero casarme con alguien de Hollywood.

_____ 4. Me enojo con personas que no me dicen la verdad.

_____ 5. Cuando una persona me miente, generalmente rompo con él o con ella.

_____ 6. Por las mañanas me basta con tomar café.

_____ 7. Sueño con ser una estrella de cine algún día.

_____ 8. Siempre puedo contar con mi mejor amigo/a.

_____ 9. Me junto con muchos músicos.

_____ 10. No me asocio con vendedores de drogas ni de pistolas.

_____ 11. Me aburro con la mayoría de los programas en la televisión.

_____ 12. Cuando no hay luces, a veces me tropiezo con el sofá.

_____ 13. Cuando estoy enojado/a, amenazo con matar a alguien.

_____ 14. Muchas compañías de los Estados Unidos comercian con Japón.

_____ 15. Siempre me conformo con pagar los impuestos sin quejarme.

ejercicio   II-3-4

You may consult the list of verbs that require **con** as you translate these sentences.

1. You can count on me, but can I count on you? _____

2. Every Wednesday I meet up with Kay (_in order_) to eat dinner (_cenar_) and to converse.

_____

3. In the movie Superman, Clark Kent goes out with (_dates_) Lois Lane. _____

_____

4. I become afraid of the dark (_la oscuridad_) during a storm (_la tormenta_). _____

_____

5. It's tragic, but sometimes (*a veces*) a person needs to break off relations with his/her family.

_____

6. The egomaniac (*el egoísta*) dreams of being famous, popular, and rich. _____

_____

7. I don't associate with companies that sell tobacco (*el tabaco*). _____

_____

8. Now and then (*de vez en cuando*) I am mistaken about people (*la persona*). _____

_____

9. We always have a good time with our neighbors (*el vecino*). _____

_____

10. She gets angry at me when I am late (*llegar tarde*). _____

11. José has no dealings with his wife's family. _____

12. If you clean the bathtub (*la bañera*) with Brillo, you're going to damage it (*dañarla*). _____

_____

13. Now and then I come upon someone who truly (*verdaderamente*) inspires (*inspirar*) me. _____

_____

14. If Juan isn't careful (*no tener cuidado*), he's going to bump into the wall. _____

_____

15. On Sunday mornings, I often content myself with (*an*) orange juice and the newspaper.

_____

de

Verbs that are followed by **de** often are verbs of cessation or withdrawal. This is clearly seen in **terminar de** + *verb,* which means "to finish (doing something)." You will see many examples of this feeling of something ending as you examine the list of verbs.

The preposition **de** also follows many verbs of emotion. **Aburrirse de** (to be bored by/with), **cansarse de** (to be tired of), **sorprenderse de** (to be surprised at) are a few examples of verbs of emotion that take **de.**

aburrirse de *(n., v.)*	to be bored by/with (someone, something, doing something)
abusar de *(n.)*	to take advantage of, impose upon, abuse (someone, something)
acabar de *(v.)*	to have just (done something)

acordarse de *(n., v.)*	to remember (someone, something, to do something)
alegrarse de *(n., v.)*	to be glad of/about (something), to be happy to (do something)
alejarse de *(n.)*	to go/get away from (someone, something, somewhere)
aprovecharse de *(n., v.)*	to take advantage of (someone, something, doing something)
arrepentirse de *(n., v.)*	to repent, be sorry for (something, doing something)
asombrarse de *(n.)*	to be astonished at (something)
avergonzarse de *(n.)*	to be ashamed of (someone, something)
brindar a la salud de *(n.)*	to toast (someone)
burlarse de *(n.)*	to make fun of (someone, something)
cansarse de *(n., v.)*	to be/get tired of (someone, something, doing something)
carecer de *(n.)*	to lack (something)
cesar de *(v.)*	to cease (doing something)
conseguir (algo) de *(n.)*	to obtain/get (something) from (someone, something)
cuidar de *(n.)*	to care for, take care of (something)
deber de *(v.)*	to suppose [conjecture], "must be" (someone, something)
dejar de *(v.)*	to stop (doing something)
depender de *(n., v.)*	to depend on (someone, something, doing something)
encargarse de *(n., v.)*	to take charge of (someone, something, doing something)
estar encargado de *(n., v.)*	to be in charge of (someone, something, doing something)
gozar de *(n.)*	to enjoy (something)
haber de *(v.)*	to suppose [conjecture] to (be or do something)
hablar de *(n., v.)*	to talk of/about, speak of (someone, something, doing something)
jactarse de *(n., v.)*	to brag about, boast of (something, doing something)
librarse de *(n.)*	to get rid of (someone, something)
llenar(se) de *(n.)*	to fill (up) with (something)
maldecir de *(n.)*	to speak ill of (something)
maravillarse de *(n.)*	to marvel at (someone, something)
marcharse de *(n.)*	to leave, walk away from (a place)
morir de *(n.)*	to die [literally] of/from (an illness, a situation)
morirse de *(n.)*	to be dying [figuratively] for/of (something)
ocuparse de *(n., v.)*	to concern oneself with, pay attention to, deal with (someone, something, doing something)
olvidarse de *(n., v.)*	to forget (someone, something, to do something)
parar de *(v.)*	to cease, stop (doing something)
pensar de *(n.)*	to think of, have an opinion about (someone, something)
preciarse de *(n., v.)*	to brag about, boast of, pride oneself on (something, doing something)
prescindir de *(n., v.)*	to do without, neglect (someone, something, doing something)
probar de *(n.)*	to sample, take a taste of (something)
quejarse de *(n., v.)*	to complain of/about (someone, something, doing something)
salir de *(n.)*	to leave, go away from (a place)
separarse de *(n.)*	to leave, part company with (someone, something, a place)
servir de *(n.)*	to act as, serve as, be useful for (someone, something)
sorprenderse de *(n.)*	to be surprised at, be amazed at (something)
terminar de *(v.)*	to finish (doing something)
tratar de *(v.)*	to try to (do something)
tratarse de *(n., v.)*	to be a question of (something, doing something)

¿Verdadero o falso?

_____ 1. Acabo de comer una hamburguesa.

_____ 2. Usualmente, me alegro de tomar un examen.

_____ 3. Cada primavera me libro de muchas cosas que ya no necesito en mi casa.

_____ 4. Gozo mucho del teatro.

_____ 5. En mi casa estoy encargado/a de sacar la basura.

_____ 6. Parte de mi decisión de ir de vacaciones depende de la cantidad de dinero que tengo en el banco.

_____ 7. Me aburro mucho de las personas que no piensan antes de hablar.

_____ 8. Cada día trato de ser una persona honrada (*honest*).

_____ 9. Típicamente salgo de mi casa entre las siete y las nueve de la mañana.

_____ 10. Normalmente no me acuerdo de pagar las cuentas (*bills*) cada mes.

_____ 11. La fruta puede servir de ensalada o de postre.

_____ 12. A veces me olvido del nombre de una persona a quien acabo de conocer.

_____ 13. Cada año miles de personas mueren de cáncer de pulmón (*lung*).

_____ 14. Si no desayuno, para las once de la mañana me muero de hambre.

_____ 15. Muchas personas se quejan de pagar los impuestos cada 15 de abril.

ejericio   II-3-5

You may consult the list of verbs that require **de** *as you translate these sentences.*

1. He always forgets to take his medicine. _____

2. This sofa serves as a comfortable (*cómodo*) bed. _____

3. We have to finish cleaning the house by four-thirty. _____

4. Every day I get rid of at least (*por lo menos*) one thing because I don't like clutter (*el desorden*).

_____

5. She always complains about working so much (*tanto*). _____

6. I marvel at people who can dance well. _____

7. I'm in charge of cooking, and you're in charge of serving the meals. _____

_____

8. I often forget a person's name, but I never forget his face. _____

_____

9. You should get away from dangerous people. _____

10. I have just read a wonderful article (*el artículo*) in the newspaper. _____

_____

11. Don't we have orange juice? I'm dying of thirst (*la sed*). _____

_____

12. Who's going to take care of your house next week? _____

_____

13. They're talking about moving (*mudarse*) to Omaha next year. _____

_____

14. I don't like to be with him because he always speaks ill (*mal*) of other people. _____

_____

15. There are people who take advantage of others without remorse (*remordimiento*). _____

_____

en

When a Spanish verb takes the preposition **en,** that **en** often will translate in English as "in" or "on." For example, **confiar en** means "to confide in, trust"; while **insistir en** means "to insist on."

One of the more frequently used verbs in this category is **pensar en,** which usually means "to think about"; however, some English speakers use the expression "to think on." Even though some verbs in this category are idiomatic in their translation, many, under inspection, will reveal a use of *in* or *on.* The only recourse is to familiarize yourself with them and use them until you feel comfortable.

abdicar en *(n.)*	to abdicate (the throne, etc.) to (someone)
complacerse en *(n., v.)*	to take pleasure in (something, doing something)
confiar en *(n., v.)*	to trust, confide in (someone, a situation, doing something)
consentir en *(v.)*	to consent to (do something)
consistir en *(n., v.)*	to consist of (something, doing something)
convenir en *(n., v.)*	to agree to (something, do something)
convertirse en *(n.)*	to become, change into (someone, something)
empeñarse en *(n., v.)*	to insist on, persist in, get involved in (something, doing something)

equivocarse en *(n.)*	to make a mistake in (something)
esforzarse en *(n., v.)*	to try hard in (something); to endeavor to (do something)
influir en *(n.)*	to influence, have an affect on (someone, something)
insistir en *(n., v.)*	to insist on (something, doing something)
interesarse en *(n.)*	to be interested in (someone, something)
meterse en *(n., v.)*	to become involved in (something, doing something)
mojarse en *(n.)*	to get mixed up in (something)
molestarse en *(v.)*	to take the trouble to (do something)
montar en *(n.)*	to ride (something—a bicycle)
obstinarse en *(n., v.)*	to persist in (something, doing something)
ocuparse en *(n., v.)*	to be busy with (something, doing something)
parar(se) en *(n.)*	to stop at, stay at (a place)
pensar en *(n., v.)*	to think about (someone, something, doing something)
persistir en *(n., v.)*	to persist in (something, doing something)
quedar en *(n., v.)*	to agree to (something, do something)
reflexionar en *(n.)*	to reflect on, think about (something)
tardar (tiempo) en *(n., v.)*	to delay in (something, doing something), to take (time) to (do something)
trabajar en *(n.)*	to work on/at (something)
verse en *(n.)*	to find oneself in/at (a situation, a place)

¿Verdadero o falso?

_____ 1. No me gusta meterme en los problemas de los demás.

_____ 2. Huevos rancheros consiste en huevos y rancheros.

_____ 3. Yo confío en mi mejor amigo/a.

_____ 4. En el cuento "Cenicienta", los ratones se convierten en caballos.

_____ 5. La memoria de la madre Teresa influye en muchas personas por el mundo.

_____ 6. Tardo más de veinte minutos en ir de mi casa al aeropuerto.

_____ 7. Es descortés persistir en discutir algo que la otra persona no quiere discutir.

_____ 8. Pienso mucho en la Guerra Civil.

_____ 9. Siempre pienso en el bienestar (*well-being*) de otros.

_____ 10. Todos los sábados me paro en una gasolinera para comprar chicle y revistas.

_____ 11. Siempre me empeño en leer un contrato palabra por palabra antes de firmarlo.

_____ 12. Es peligroso montar en un coche con una persona que está borracha (*drunk*).

_____ 13. Las personas obsesionadas con el control siempre insisten en tener la última palabra.

_____ 14. Tengo que confesarlo: me esfuerzo en aprender a usar el Internet, pero es muy difícil.

_____ 15. Nunca quedo en hacer algo que es peligroso.

ejercicio   II-3-6

*You may consult the list of verbs that require **en** as you translate these sentences.*

1. Some people persist in exercising (*hacer ejercicio*) even (*aun*) when they're sick. _____

    _____

2. María takes pleasure in playing the guitar at parties. _____

    _____

3. First I think about food, and then I think about eating something. _____

    _____

4. Every day we should reflect on something good in (*de*) this world. _____

    _____

5. At the end (*A finales*) of the month, Marcos always finds himself in a jam (*el apuro*). _____

    _____

6. When the police arrive, the thief consents to go with them peacefully (*pacíficamente*). _____

    _____

7. People who gossip (*chismear*) involve themselves in other people's lives. _____

    _____

8. Juan and María agree to consult a psychiatrist (*el psiquiatra*). _____

    _____

9. Every year I agree to contribute (*donar*) to the Cancer Society. _____

    _____

10. You shouldn't get involved in their problems. _____

11. I'm not thinking about anything now. _____

12. My sister never takes the trouble to telephone (*llamar por teléfono*). _____

    _____

13. I am very interested in international politics (*la política internacional*). _____

    _____

14. It takes me one hour to drive to the stadium (*el estadio*) from here. _____

_____

15. For exercise, the children ride bicycles. _____

para

The smallest group of verbs that take a preposition consists of the verbs that take **para.** The preposition **para** often implies moving ahead or toward something. Recall that a good image for **para** is an arrow because it moves straight ahead. As you will see, the following verbs indicate that an action is occurring for the purpose of something else to happen: one thing moves ahead, precipitating something else.

estar listo/a para *(v.)*	to be ready to (do something)
estar para *(v.)*	to be about to (do something)
quedarse para *(v.)*	to stay to (do something)
prepararse para *(n., v.)*	to prepare oneself (for something, to do something)
sentarse para *(v.)*	to sit down to (do something)
servir para *(n., v.)*	to be of use for, serve as (something, doing something)
trabajar para *(n., v.)*	to work for (someone, a company); to strive to (do something)

¿Verdadero o falso?

_____ 1. Trabajo para una persona muy simpática y honrada.

_____ 2. Cuando me siento para comer, generalmente tengo conmigo un periódico o una revista.

_____ 3. Para mí, la televisión no sirve para nada.

_____ 4. Estoy listo/a para tomar el examen final en esta clase de español.

_____ 5. Cada mañana me preparo para el trabajo.

_____ 6. Un diccionario de español sirve para enseñar el idioma.

_____ 7. Cuando estoy para dormir, enciendo todas las luces en la casa.

_____ 8. Cada día trabajo para mejorarme y entender más del mundo.

_____ 9. Un buen negociante se queda en la oficina para terminar el trabajo cada noche.

_____ 10. Cuando me preparo para acostarme, siempre me cepillo los dientes.

_____ 11. El anillo de matrimonio sirve para simbolizar el compromiso (*commitment*).

_____ 12. Un contable (*accountant*) trabaja para ahorrar (*to save*) dinero para su cliente.

ejercicio   II-3-7

You may consult the list of verbs that require **para** *as you translate these sentences.*

1. Usually it's very late when I sit down to study. _____

2. Martha Stewart says that many things in the garbage can (*la basura*) serve as decorations in the house.

   _____

3. A: Are you ready to leave? B: Yes, we're ready to leave. _____

   _____

4. We're about to eat lunch (*almorzar*). _____

5. I want to work for another company. _____

6. Do you want to stay to watch the news (*las noticias*) with me? _____

   _____

7. This film is of no use. _____

8. Every January many people strive to lose weight (*perder peso*). _____

   _____

9. Melissa needs at least (*por lo menos*) two hours in order to prepare herself for her date (*la cita*).

   _____

10. Bjorn is preparing himself to find a new job because he works for a real brute (*el bruto*). _____

    _____

por

Verbs that take *por* often deal with emotions (see **llorar por**) or convey a feeling of equality, in the sense of *on behalf of* (see **abogar por**). Emotions and equality are the two main categories covered when studying **por.**

You can see the difference that **para** (purpose and destination) and **por** (emotions and equality) make with regard to verbs in the verb pairs **estar *para*** (to be about to do something) and **estar *por*** (to be in favor of), as well as **trabajar *para*** (to work for someone) and **trabajar *por*** (to work in place of or on behalf of someone).

abogar por (*n.*)	to plead on behalf of (someone, something)
acabar por (*v.*)	to end by, wind up (doing something)
apurarse por (*n., v.*)	to worry oneself about, fret over (someone, something, doing something)

cambiar por *(n.)*   to exchange (something); to change (something) into (something)
clasificar por *(n.)*   to classify in/by (something)
dar gracias por *(n., v.)*   to thank for, give thanks for (something, doing something)
esforzarse por *(n., v.)*   to strive for (someone, something, doing something)
estar por *(v.)*   to be inclined to (do something), be in favor of (doing something)
hacer por *(v.)*   to try to (do something)
impacientarse por *(n., v.)*   to grow impatient for, be impatient to (someone, something, do something)
llorar por *(n., v.)*   to cry for/about (someone, something, doing something)
luchar por *(n., v.)*   to struggle for (someone, something, doing something)
mandar por *(n.)*   to send via (something—mail)
mirar por *(n.)*   to care about, worry about (someone)
morirse por *(n., v.)*   to be dying for (something, doing something)
ofenderse por *(n., v.)*   to be offended by (something, doing something)
optar por *(n., v.)*   to choose, opt for (something, doing something)
preocuparse por *(n., v.)*   to worry about (someone, something, doing something)
rabiar por *(n., v.)*   to be crazy about (someone, something, doing something)
terminar por *(v.)*   to end by (doing something)
trabajar por *(n.)*   to work for (someone—as a substitute)
votar por *(n.)*   to vote for (someone, something)

¿Verdadero o falso?

_____ 1. Me preocupo mucho por el dinero.

_____ 2. Cuando tengo que decidir entre la televisión o el teatro, usualmente opto por el teatro.

_____ 3. Perry Mason aboga por sus clientes.

_____ 4. Las personas de Argentina lloran por Evita Perón.

_____ 5. En las elecciones políticas, siempre voto por el candidato más moderado.

_____ 6. Romeo rabia por Julieta.

_____ 7. Puedo comprar más si cambio mis dólares por pesos.

_____ 8. Durante los fines de semana, estoy por dormir mucho y trabajar poco.

_____ 9. A veces doy gracias por las dificultades de la vida.

_____ 10. Cuando un maestro está enfermo, típicamente un sustituto trabaja por él.

_____ 11. Con frecuencia la orquesta termina por tocar algo excepcional.

_____ 12. Si no tengo planes específicos para el fin de semana, usualmente acabo por no hacer nada.

_____ 13. Me esfuerzo por hacer lo mejor que pueda todos los días.

_____ 14. Me impaciento por personas que conducen muy lentamente.

_____ 15. Durante el año, mando muchos regalos por correo.

ejercicio II-3-8

*You may consult the list of verbs that require **por** as you translate these sentences.*

1. Harold worries about losing his teeth and his hair. _____

2. In the novel *Anna Karenina*, Levin struggles always to do the right thing (*lo correcto*). _____

_____

3. The people (*el pueblo*) of Argentina shouldn't cry for Evita. _____

4. I care (*worry*) a lot about you. _____

5. Many people are offended by the waste (*el desperdicio*) of food in restaurants. _____

_____

6. I'm dying to see your new hairdo (*el peinado*). _____

7. In this office, we classify everything by size (*el tamaño*). _____

8. Usually a gymnast (*el gimnasta*) ends by doing something spectacular (*espectacular*). _____

_____

9. They always opt for swimming in the river. _____

10. When I have a choice (*la elección*) between two movies, I usually opt for the (*one*) that has the

better reviews (*la reseña*). _____

11. Laura is impatient to move (*mudarse*) to another part of the country. _____

_____

12. Many lawyers plead on behalf of a guilty (*culpable*) person. _____

13. We give you thanks for telling us the truth. _____

14. I always classify my books alphabetically (*orden alfabético*). _____

15. She always votes for the less attractive candidate. _____

PART III

Appendices

The Eight Parts of Speech

1. Noun: A word that represents a person, place, thing, or idea

   boss **jefe**   house **casa**

   pencil **lápiz**   liberty **libertad**

2. Verb: A word that expresses an action, occurrence, or mode of being

   jump **saltar**   rain **llover**   be **ser**

3. Adjective: A word that modifies or describes a noun. It can be descriptive or quantitative. (See the comment on articles below.)

   Descriptive:

   big **grande**   tall **alto**   beautiful **bello**

   Quantitative:

   several **varios**   many **muchos**   two **dos**

4. Adverb: A word that modifies or describes a verb, an adjective, or another adverb

   there **allí**   very **muy**   slowly **lentamente**

5. Preposition: A word or phrase that functions to show the relationship between two words in a phrase, clause, or sentence

   of **de**   between **entre**   for **para**

6. Interjection: A word or phrase used as an exclamation without any grammatical function

   Great! **¡Maravilloso!**   Darn! **¡Caramba!**

7. Pronoun: A word used in place of a noun that is understood either through use previously or through context

   he **él**   our **nuestro**   no one **nadie**

8. Conjunction: A word or phrase that connects sentences, clauses, phrases, or words

   and **y**   neither . . . nor **ni . . . ni**

Articles: Classified as definite and indefinite. Technically, articles are adjectives because they qualify nouns; however, many people believe that they deserve separate status due to their frequency of use.

the **el, la**   a, an **un, una**

Pronoun Definitions and Charts

1. Personal (or Subject) Pronouns

   A personal or subject pronoun replaces an understood noun that denotes the actor (performer/agent) in a sentence:

   Yo comí un durazno, pero **tú** comiste toda la sandía.
   I ate a peach, but *you* ate all the watermelon.

Singular	Plural
yo (I)	**nosotros** (we—masc./masc. & fem.) **nosotras** (we—fem. only)
tú (you—familiar)	**vosotros** (you—familiar; masc./ masc. & fem.) **vosotras** (you—familiar; fem. only)
él (he) **ella** (she) **usted** (you—formal)	**ellos** (they—masc./masc. & fem.) **ellas** (they—fem. only) **ustedes** (you—formal)

2. Interrogative Pronouns

An interrogative pronoun is used in asking questions. The answer sought will be a noun (either a thing or the name of a person) or a pronoun:

¿Quién está en la cárcel?   **¿Cuál** prefieres?
Who is in jail?   *Which* do you prefer?

¿Quién? ¿Quiénes?	Who?
¿A quién? ¿A quiénes?	(To) Whom?
¿De quién? ¿De quiénes?	Whose?
¿Qué?	What? (Which?)
¿Cuál? ¿Cuáles?	Which? (What?)

3. Pronouns as Objects of Prepositions

A word that follows a preposition is called the object of the preposition. Pronouns that follow prepositions are almost identical to the subject pronouns, with the exceptions of *mí* and *ti* and the addition of the third-person neuter form of *ello*.

para mí   a usted   cerca de ella
for me   to you   near her

Singular	Plural
mí (me)	**nosotros** (us—masc./masc. & fem.) **nosotras** (us—fem. only)
ti (you—familiar)	**vosotros** (you—familiar; masc./ masc. & fem.) **vosotras** (you—familiar; fem. only)
él (him) **ella** (her; it, fem.) **usted** (you—formal) **ello** (it, m.; neut.)	**ellos** (them; it) **ellas** (them; it) **ustedes** (you—formal)

Pronouns with *con:* Certain pronouns that follow the preposition *con* (with) take on a special form. They are as follows:

Singular	Plural
conmigo (with me) **contigo** (with you) **consigo** (with him; with her; with you) or **con él** (with him) **con ella** (with her, it) **con usted** (with you) **con ello** (with it)	**con nosotros/as** (with us) **con vosotros/as** (with you) **consigo** (with them; with you) or **con ellos** (with them) **con ellas** (with them) **con ustedes** (with you)

Six Special Prepositions: In Spanish, six prepositions are followed by a subject pronoun, rather than an object pronoun:

entre	between	**excepto**	except
incluso	including	**menos**	except
según	according to	**salvo**	except

Reflexive Pronouns Following a Preposition: Expressing a reflexive action (an action that "reflects" back on the performer) can by done by using a preposition followed by a reflexive object pronoun.

a mí mismo	to myself	**a nosotros mismos**	to ourselves
a mí misma	to myself	**a nosotras mismas**	to ourselves
a ti mismo	to yourself	**a vosotros mismos**	to yourselves
a ti misma	to yourself	**a vosotras mismas**	to yourselves
a sí mismo/a	to himself/herself, ourself, itself	**a sí mismos/as**	to themselves, yourselves

4. Possessive Pronouns

Possessive pronouns denote ownership by an understood person or thing:

El sapo es **mío.**   Una amiga **tuya** canta muy bien.
The toad is *mine.*   A friend of *yours* sings very well.

Singular	Plural
mío(s) (mine) **mía(s)** (mine)	**nuestro(s)** (ours) **nuestra(s)** (ours)
tuyo(s) (yours) **tuya(s)** (yours)	**vuestro(s)** (yours) **vuestra(s)** (yours)
suyo(s) (his; hers; yours; its) **suya(s)** (his; hers; yours; its)	**suyo(s)** (theirs; yours) **suya(s)** (theirs; yours)

5. Demonstrative Pronouns

Demonstrative pronouns "point out" understood persons, places, or things:

Me gustan las dos camisas, pero prefiero **ésa.**
I like both shirts, but I prefer *that one.*

	Masculine	Feminine	Neuter
this these	**éste** **éstos**	**ésta** **éstas**	**esto**
that those	**ése** **ésos**	**ésa** **ésas**	**eso**
that over there those over there	**aquél** **aquéllos**	**aquélla** **aquéllas**	**aquello**

6. Numbers as Pronouns

When the noun is understood, the number itself—whether cardinal or ordinal—will carry its meaning and stand for the noun, thus functioning as a pronoun:

Las tortitas son deliciosas. Dame **una,** por favor.
The cupcakes are delicious. Give me *one,* please.

De todos los coches que probamos, me gusta más el **segundo.**
Of all the cars we tried out, I like the *second* one best.

Cardinal Numbers	Ordinal Numbers
uno/a	**primero/a**
dos	**segundo/a**
tres	**tercero/a**
cuatro	**cuarto/a**
cinco	**quinto/a**
seis	**sexto/a**
siete	**séptimo/a**
ocho	**octavo/a**
nueve	**noveno/a**
diez	**décimo/a**

7. Adjectives as Pronouns

In Spanish, an adjective (or past participle) can function as a pronoun. In other words, it can stand for a noun that is understood or that has been stated.

¡Anoche Carmen salió con un **anciano!** [*hombre* is understood]
Last night Carmen went out with an *old man!*

Tú compraste los platos azules, pero yo compré los **blancos.** [*platos* is previously stated]
You bought the blue plates, but I bought the *white.*

In Spanish, many quantitative adjective pronouns correspond to indefinite pronouns in English. Others are adjectives with "clipped," or omitted, words.

Nadie vino a la fiesta.
No one came to the party.

Te di tu invitación, pero mandé **las demás** por correo.
I gave you your invitation, but I sent *the rest* by mail.

The following are commonly used quantitative adjectives and adjective pronouns:

algo	something; anything
alguien	somebody; someone
algunos/as	some (of them); any (of them)
ambos/as	both
cada	each
cada uno/a	each one
cualquiera	anyone; anybody; any one (person); anything; whichever; whatever
cualesquiera	any people (*pl.*); any (*pl.*)
demasiado/a	too much
demasiados/as	too many
el/la mayor	the oldest/eldest (one)
el/la menor	the youngest (one)
lo mejor	the best (thing)
lo mismo	the same (thing)
lo peor	the worst (thing)
los/las dos	both
los otros, las otras	the others
mucho/a	much; a lot of
muchos/as	many; a lot of
nada	nothing
nadie	nobody; no one (person)
ninguno/a	none; not anything; neither one
otro/a	another; the other
poco/a	(a) little
pocos/as	few
todo	everything; all
todos/as	everyone; everybody
último/a	last
unos/as	some
unos cuantos, unas cuantas	a few (of them)
varios/as	several

8. Relative Pronouns

A relative pronoun connects a dependent clause with a principal clause:

Las personas **que** viven allí son muy simpáticas.
The people *who* live there are very nice.

Ella es la señora con **quien** trabajo.
She is the lady with *whom* I work.

Lo **que** debes hacer es ganar la lotería.
What you should do is win the lottery.

The following are commonly used relative pronouns:

cuyo, cuya, cuyos, cuyas	whose
el cual, la cual	the one who; the one which
el que, la que	the one who; the one which
lo que	that which; what; whatever
los cuales, las cuales	those who; the ones which
los que, las que	those who; those which
que	that; who; which; that/which (following a preposition)
quien, quienes	whom (following a preposition)

9. Direct Object Pronouns

A pronoun that names the receiver or the result of the action expressed by the verb is the direct object pronoun. It answers the question What? or Whom?

¿Ese libro? **Lo** leí. ¿Cuándo vas a leer**lo** tú?
That book? I read *it*. When are you going to read *it*?

Tú ya no **me** amas, pero yo sigo queriéndo**te**.
You don't love *me* anymore, but I still love *you*.

Singular	Plural
me (me)	**nos** (us)
te (you)	**os** (you all)
lo (him; you; it)	**los** (them; you)
la (her; you; it)	**las** (them; you)

10. Indirect Object Pronouns

A pronoun that denotes to or for whom or which something is done is an indirect object pronoun. It answers the question To or for whom? or To or for what?

Juan siempre **le** da una rosa blanca a María.
Juan always gives *María* a white rose.

¡No **me** digas mentiras!
Don't tell *me* lies!

No he oído el último chiste. Cuénta**me**lo, por favor.
I haven't heard the latest joke. Tell it to *me*, please.

Singular	Plural
me (me)	**nos** (us)
te (you)	**os** (you all)
le (him; her; it; you)	**les** (them; you)

11. Reflexive Object Pronouns

A pronoun that indicates that the agent and the recipient of an action are the same person (or thing) is a reflexive object pronoun.

Me veo en el espejo.
I see myself in the mirror.

Nos cepillamos los dientes tres veces al día.
We brush our teeth three times a day.

Singular	Plural
me (myself) **te** (yourself) **se** (himself; herself; itself; yourself)	**nos** (ourselves) **os** (yourselves) **se** (themselves; yourselves)

12. RID: Reflexive, Indirect, and Direct Object Pronouns

RID is a handy acronym to remember when there are two object pronouns in a sentence. The order in the sentence is always **reflexive** pronoun, **indirect** object pronoun, **direct** object pronoun.

Me encanta tu pelo. ¿**Te** [R] **lo** [D] lavas mucho?
I love your hair. Do you wash **it** a lot?

Él no sabe la verdad. **Se** [I] **la** [D] debemos decir.
He doesn't know the truth. We should tell **it to him.**

In the last example, the indirect and the direct object pronouns can also be attached to the infinitive: *Debemos decírsela*. Note that an accent mark is usually added to retain the original stress in the infinitive. Also note that whenever the two object pronouns begin with the letter *l*, the *l* in the first pronoun changes to *s*. Instead of *Le la debemos decir*, you say, *Se la debemos decir.*

R + D + conjugated verb
or
infinitive + R + D

I + D + conjugated verb
or
infinitive + I + D

13. Reciprocal Pronouns

A pronoun that expresses reciprocity, or an action "going both ways" between the subjects, is a reciprocal pronoun.

Nos conocimos ayer.
We met each other yesterday.

Se hablan mucho.
They talk to one another a lot.

nos (each other; each of us; one another) **os** (each other; each of you; one another) **se** (each other; each of them; each of you; one another)

14. Uses of **se**

Se is commonly used to express the passive voice in Spanish.

La cena **se comió** junto al lago.
Dinner *was eaten* by the lake.

Se also is used to express an unknown, impersonal subject.
En este colegio **se estudia** mucho.

In this high school, *one studies* a lot.
In this high school, *they study* a lot.

¡No **se debe** fumar nunca!
One should never smoke!
You should never smoke!

Often actions involving inanimate objects also employ *se:*

Mi coche **se** me **descompone** todo el tiempo.
My car *breaks down* on me all the time.

Los cristales **se quebraron** cuando ella cantó.
The glassware *broke* when she sang.

se + (third-person) conjugated verb

Prepositions

Prepositions That Show Relationship

about	acerca de
about, on (topic)	sobre
according to	según
against	contra
besides, in addition to	además de
except	excepto, menos, salvo
instead of	en vez de, en lugar de
with	con
without	sin

Prepositions of Physical Location

above	sobre
across	a través de
across from, opposite	enfrente de
among	entre (varias cosas o personas)
at	a, en
behind	detrás de
between	entre (dos cosas o personas)
by	de
facing	frente a

far from	lejos de
in	en
in front (of)	delante (de)
inside	dentro de
near, close to	cerca de
next to, next door (to)	al lado (de), junto (a)
on	en
on top of	encima de, sobre
outside	fuera de
to the left (of)	a la izquierda (de)
to the right (of)	a la derecha (de)
under	debajo de
with	con

Prepositions of Movement

along	a lo largo de
around	alrededor de
backward(s)	hacia atrás
beyond	más allá de
forward(s)	hacia adelante
sideways	de lado
through, throughout	por
toward	hacia

Prepositions of Geographical Location

to the north of	al norte de
to the south of	al sur de
to the east of	al este de
to the west of	al oeste de
to the northeast of	al nordeste de
to the northwest of	al noroeste de
to the southeast of	al sudeste (sureste) de
to the southwest of	al sudoeste (suroeste) de

Prepositions of Origin and Destination
Origin

because of, for	a causa de, por
by	por, de (to indicate authorship)
(all the way) from	desde
from	de
of	de

Destination

for (purpose/destination)	para
to	a
toward	hacia

Prepositions of Time

after	después de
afterwards	después
before	antes de
beforehand	antes

during	durante
since	desde
through	por
to, until	a
until	hasta

The Uses of *Para* and *Por*

Para
1. Destination
   a. Indicates real or figurative destination
   b. Expresses the recipient of an action
   c. Indicates direction and/or final travel destination
   d. Indicates aim or objective of an action (+ profession)
2. Purpose
   a. Expresses purpose (before an infinitive)
   b. Tells why one does something; "in order to" (before an infinitive)
3. Deadline
   a. Expresses a specific time limit or deadline (in the future)
   b. Expresses a limited timespan in the future
4. Standard
   a. Expresses a comparison to a certain standard
   b. Expresses an opinion or personal standard

Por
1. Duration
   a. Expresses duration of time
   b. Indicates periods of time during the 24-hour day
   c. Expresses the English use of the Latin *per*
2. Substitution or Exchange
   a. Indicates an equal exchange or trade
   b. Expresses substitution ("in behalf of," "in place of")
   c. Expresses thanks and gratitude
3. Motivation
   a. Indicates having done something or "because of" (*por* + infinitive)
   b. Expresses a motive for doing something
   c. Tells why something or someone is a certain way (*por* + noun or infinitive)
4. Movement
   a. Expresses means of transportation
   b. Expresses means of sending messages or information
   c. Indicates the point of a temporary stop
   d. Indicates movement in an area
5. Emotions
   a. Expresses a liking (or disliking) or an emotion for someone or something
6. Appears in idiomatic expressions

Answer Key

Unit 1: Subject Pronouns

ejercicio   I-1-1

1. yo
2. nosotros/as
3. ellos (ellas; ustedes)
4. él (ella; usted)
5. vosotros/as
6. nosotros/as
7. él (ella; usted)

8. ellos (ellas; ustedes)
9. vosotros/as
10. tú
11. él (ella; usted)
12. yo
13. tú
14. vosotros/as

15. él (ella; usted)
16. yo
17. tú
18. nosotros/as
19. ellos (ellas; ustedes)
20. tú

ejercicio   I-1-2

1. yo tengo
2. tú tienes
3. él quiere
4. nosotros estamos
5. vosotros/as salís
6. ustedes (ellos; ellas) quieren
7. yo puedo

8. ella viene
9. nosotros/as somos
10. tú sales
11. usted juega
12. yo pongo
13. ustedes ponen
14. ellos dicen

15. vosotros/as estáis
16. tú oyes
17. ellas pueden
18. nosotros vemos
19. nosotros/as oímos
20. vosotros/as veis

Unit 2: Interrogative Pronouns

ejercicio   I-2-1

1. ¿Quién es ella?
2. ¿Quiénes son ellos?
3. ¿Quién eres? ¿Quién es usted?
4. ¿Quiénes sois? ¿Quiénes son ustedes?
5. ¿Quién trabaja aquí?

6. ¿Quién mira la televisión?
7. ¿Quién habla español aquí?
8. ¿Quién no vive aquí?
9. ¿Quién escribe el libro?
10. ¿Quién es tu/su amigo?

ejercicio   I-2-2

1. ¿A quién amas?
2. ¿A quién ves?
3. ¿A quién miras?
4. ¿A quiénes miras?

5. ¿A quién buscas?
6. ¿A quiénes buscas?
7. ¿A quién escuchas?

8. ¿A quiénes escuchas?
9. ¿A quién conoces?
10. ¿A quiénes conoces?

ejercicio   I-2-3

1. ¿De quién es este coche?
2. ¿De quién son las llaves que están en la mesa?
3. ¿De quiénes son los coches que están sucios?
4. ¿De quiénes son las niñas que leen estos libros?
5. ¿De quién es el gato que bebe la leche?
6. ¿De quién son los vecinos que viven en la casa azul?
7. ¿De quiénes son los estudiantes más inteligentes?
8. ¿De quién es el coche que no funciona?
9. ¿De quién es este abrigo?
10. ¿De quién es el loro que habla italiano?
11. ¿De quiénes son estos casetes?
12. ¿De quién es esta mochila?

ejercicio   I-2-4

1. ¿Qué libro es más interesante?
2. ¿Qué actor es más popular?
3. ¿Qué chica es tu prima?
4. ¿Qué comida tiene más grasa?
5. ¿Qué tienda vende más ropa?
6. ¿Cuál comes más, el pollo o el pescado?
7. ¿Cuál es más popular?
8. ¿Cuál es tu nombre?
9. ¿Cuál es tu dirección?
10. ¿Cuáles llevas más?
11. ¿Qué zapatos llevas más?
12. ¿Qué sombrero es más cómodo?
13. ¿Cuál de los sombreros es más cómodo?
14. ¿Qué programa miras?
15. ¿Cuáles de los nuevos programas miras?
16. ¿Cuáles miras?

ejercicio   I-2-5

1. ¿Qué día es hoy?
2. ¿Cuál es la fecha de hoy?
3. ¿Cuál es su nombre?
4. ¿Qué hora es?
5. ¿Cuál es tu razón por esto?
6. ¿Qué es eso?
7. ¿Qué libro quieres tú?
8. ¿Cuáles quieres?
9. ¿Qué mujer es tu amiga?
10. ¿Qué significa esto?
11. ¿Cuál es la respuesta?
12. ¿Qué quieres saber?

Unit 3: Pronouns as Objects of Prepositions

ejercicio   I-3-1

1. Él tiene un libro para mí.
2. Tengo un regalo para ti.
3. ¿Qué tienes para mí?
4. La mesa es de ella.
5. Compro mis libros de ellos.
6. Él está delante de ello.
7. Estás detrás de él.
8. Él vive cerca de mí.
9. La alfombra está debajo de nosotras.
10. Él vive cerca de ustedes (vosotros/as).
11. Él escribe un libro acerca de ella.
12. Caminamos detrás de ellos.
13. Ella baila a la derecha de mí.
14. Ellos trabajan a la izquierda de ti.
15. La comida está delante de nosotros.

ejercicio   I-3-2

1. Estoy contigo.
2. Usted está conmigo.
3. Ella está con él.
4. Él está con ella.
5. Trabajo contigo ahora.
6. Ellos viven conmigo.
7. ¿Estudia ella contigo?
8. ¿Quién vive con ustedes?
9. ¿Por qué no bailas con él?
10. Quiero hablar con usted.

11. Él vive con nosotros.
12. Ella siempre lleva las llaves consigo.
13. Ellos nunca llevan las llaves consigo.

14. Martín está conmigo.
15. ¿Por qué (usted) no lleva el paraguas consigo?
16. ¿Por qué (ellas) no llevan el paraguas consigo?

ejercicio   I-3-3

1. Hay veinte personas aquí, incluso tú y yo.
2. Según ella, el dinero puede comprar la felicidad.
3. Entre tú, yo y el piano de cola, esta pintura es espantosa.
4. Creo que todo el mundo habla francés aquí menos (excepto; salvo) yo.
5. Entre nosotros y ellos, tenemos suficiente dinero.
6. Todos aquí están escandalizados, incluso yo.
7. Todos en la vecindad tienen una piscina salvo (menos; excepto) nosotros.
8. Tenemos muchas dificultades, según yo.
9. Todos están listos, excepto (menos; salvo) usted.
10. Según ellos, es posible vivir en Marte.

ejercicio   I-3-4

1. Compro el coche para mí mismo/a.
2. Él hace todo para sí mismo.
3. Ellos hacen todo por sí mismos.
4. Ella perjudica a sí misma cuando dice una mentira.
5. Sólo perjudicáis a vosotros/as mismos/as.
6. Escribo notas a mí mismo/a para recordar las cosas que necesito hacer.
7. Debes tener tiempo para ti mismo/a cada día.
8. Ella siempre compra un regalo para sí misma en su cumpleaños.
9. Cuando viajo, envío (mando) mis compras a mí mismo/a por correo.
10. Usted no puede vender su casa a sí mismo/a. ¡Es ridículo!

traducción   I-3-5

Pedro es mi amigo. Estoy muy feliz porque vive al lado de mí. Un mapache vive debajo de mi casa. Entre ustedes (vosotros) y yo, creo que los mapaches son animales interesantes. Leo (Estoy leyendo) un libro acerca de ellos ahora. Usualmente el mapache vive en un árbol, pero tengo suerte porque mi casa está encima de este mapache. Según Pedro, el mapache es parte de la familia del oso, y él cree que si ve el animal delante de él, es adiós, mundo. Cuando Pedro sale de o entra en mi casa, siempre mira a la izquierda y después a la derecha.

Unit 4: Possessive Pronouns

ejercicio   I-4-1

1. Es mío.
2. Es tuya.
3. Es suyo.
4. Son míos.
5. Son suyos.
6. Es nuestra.
7. Son tuyas.
8. Son vuestros.
9. Son suyas.
10. Es vuestra.
11. Son mías.
12. Son tuyas.
13. Son nuestras.
14. Es suya.
15. Son suyas.

ejercicio   I-4-2

1. El gato es mío. / Los gatos son míos.
2. La culebra es tuya (vuestra; suya). / Las culebras son tuyas (vuestras; suyas).
3. El pájaro es suyo. / Los pájaros son suyos.
4. El mono es suyo. / Los monos son suyos.
5. La jirafa es nuestra. / Las jirafas son nuestras.
6. El cerdo es suyo. / Los cerdos son suyos.
7. La araña es mía. / Las arañas son mías.
8. El caballo es tuyo (vuestro; suyo). / Los caballos son tuyos (vuestros; suyos).
9. La mariposa es suya. / Las mariposas son suyas.
10. El elefante es nuestro. / Los elefantes son nuestros.

ejercicio   I-4-3

1. Un amigo mío trabaja aquí.
2. Una amiga mía vive aquí.
3. Algunos (Unos) amigos míos tienen una cabaña en Canadá.
4. Una amiga suya estudia español.
5. Trabajo con una amiga tuya.
6. Un colega nuestro habla alemán y gaélico.
7. Ellos no quieren hablar con él porque es un enemigo suyo.
8. Un amigo tuyo es un amigo mío.
9. Esas pinturas suyas son encantadoras.
10. Una prima nuestra es una princesa en Europa.

ejercicio   I-4-4

1. Su casa está sucia, pero la nuestra está limpia.
2. Sus libros están en la cocina y los míos están en el comedor.
3. Él guarda su dinero en el banco, pero (yo) guardo el mío en el colchón.
4. Sus primos viven en Hollywood y los suyos viven en Seattle.
5. Nuestro perro es un perro pastor, y el suyo es un perro de lana.
6. Sus joyas son imitaciones, pero las mías son auténticas.
7. Ellos compran la comida en el supermercado, pero (nosotros) cultivamos la nuestra.
8. Su abogado trabaja para una firma grande. El nuestro tiene una oficina en un sótano.
9. Es mi vida. No es la tuya.
10. Vosotros tenéis vuestros problemas y yo tengo los míos.

ejercicio   I-4-5

1. Su casa es más grande que la mía.
2. Mi casa no es tan grande como la suya.
3. Su ropa es más cara (costosa) que la mía.
4. Vuestras joyas son más elegantes que las nuestras.
5. Su hurón no es tan amable como el nuestro.
6. Su termo no está tan lleno como el mío.
7. El reportaje de María es más interesante que el suyo.
8. El coche de Juan es más nuevo que el suyo.
9. Sus sobres son más bonitos que los míos. Voy a comprar una caja.
10. Sus martillos no son tan pesados como los tuyos.

ejercicio 1-4-6

1. Tu coche es mejor que el mío.
2. Sus sillas son mejores que las nuestras.
3. Mi pintura es peor que la suya.
4. Los muebles de Elena son peores que los suyos.
5. Su amigo es mayor que el mío.

6. Mis abuelos son mayores que los tuyos.
7. Nuestro hijo es menor que el vuestro.
8. Nuestras carpas doradas son menores que las suyas.
9. La paella de Julia es mejor que la mía.
10. La música de Beethoven es mejor que la suya.

traducción 1-4-7

Estoy muy disgustado/a porque Silvia tiene mi anillo. Ella dice que es suyo, pero yo sé que es mío porque tiene mis iniciales. Silvia es cleptómana. Nada en su casa es suya. Muchas cosas son mías. Por ejemplo, todas las pinturas son mías, el reloj de péndulo es mío, el candelabro en el comedor es mío, la lavadora y la secadora son mías, hasta la comida en el refrigerador es mía. ¿Qué puedo hacer? Perry Mason dice que la posesión es el noventa y nueve por ciento de la ley. Por eso, todo es suyo.

Unit 5: Demonstrative Pronouns

ejercicio 1-5-1

1. Este libro es mío, pero ése es suyo.
2. Esta casa es bonita, pero ésa es más bonita.
3. Estos zapatos son míos y ésos son suyos.
4. Estas sillas son suyas y ésas son mías.
5. Aquel chico es mi vecino y éste es mi hijo.
6. Estas mujeres son mis vecinas, pero aquéllas son de otra ciudad.
7. Ese coche es de Juan y aquél es mío.
8. Estas revistas son terribles, pero éstas son mucho mejores.
9. Este teléfono funciona, pero aquél nunca funciona.
10. Estos programas son terribles, pero ésos son aún peores.

ejercicio 1-5-2

1. ¡Esto es fantástico!
2. ¿Qué es esto?
3. Eso es un crimen.
4. Yo nunca hago eso.
5. Esto es un pecado.

6. ¿Qué pasa con aquello?
7. Por eso debes votar.
8. Esto es por qué no debo fumar.
9. ¿Quién dice eso?
10. ¿Quién escribió esto?

traducción 1-5-3

"¿Quién necesita esto? ¡Esto es tan estúpido! No necesito esto para mi trabajo." Algunas personas dicen esto cuando están frustradas o cuando tienen que tomar una clase en la universidad que no quieren tomar. Es esta clase o ésa. Es este profesor o ése. Son estos libros o ésos. Son estas tareas o ésas. ¿Cuándo termina esto? ¿Termina esto después de la graduación? Desgraciadamente, no. Esto es a menudo una actitud para la vida.

Unit 6: Numbers as Pronouns

ejercicio   I-6-1

1. A: ¿Cuántos coches tienes? B: Tengo uno.
2. A: ¿Cuántas casas tienes? B: Tengo una.
3. A: ¿Cuántas galletas quieres? B: Quiero diez.
4. A: ¿Cuántas hamburguesas quieren? B: Jane quiere dos y yo quiero una.
5. A: ¿Cuántas personas hay en tu familia? B: Hay tres.
6. Él tiene siete perros, pero yo sólo tengo seis.
7. Él ve muchas estrellas en el cielo, pero yo veo sólo una.
8. María conoce todas estas pinturas, pero nosotros conocemos sólo una.
9. Tengo sólo un teléfono, pero uno es mejor que nada.
10. A: ¿Cuántos naipes quieres? B: Quiero uno.

ejercicio   I-6-2

1. el séptimo
2. la segunda
3. el noveno
4. el quinto
5. la décima
6. el primero
7. la octava
8. la tercera
9. el sexto
10. la cuarta

ejercicio   I-6-3

1. Yo vivo en la segunda casa a la izquierda y Miguel vive en la sexta.
2. A: ¿Quién vive en la octava casa? B: No sé, pero Marcos vive en la séptima.
3. Mi coche es el tercero a la derecha, y el coche de Ricardo es el cuarto.
4. La Biblia dice que Adán es la primera persona y que Eva es la segunda.
5. La primera película siempre es mejor que la segunda.
6. La tercera película del actor es mejor que la cuarta.
7. Su quinto libro es más interesante que el sexto.
8. En España, el primer día de la semana es lunes y el séptimo es domingo.
9. El octavo mes es agosto, el noveno es septiembre y el décimo es octubre.
10. El primer enigma es más difícil que el segundo.
11. Hoy es el primero de abril.
12. La primera vez siempre es mejor que la segunda, la tercera y así sucesivamente.

traducción   I-6-4

Cuando comemos juntos, mi amigo y yo competimos para ver quién puede comer más. Por ejemplo, cuando comemos galletas, si yo como una, él come dos. Entonces yo como tres y él come cuatro. El primer participante que termina todas las galletas es el ganador. Esto es fácil con galletas o uvas o cerezas. Pero es muy difícil con hamburguesas. La primera está sabrosa. La segunda, también. La tercera no está mal. La cuarta es un reto. La quinta es absurda, también la sexta, la séptima y la octava. La novena es pura tortura. Y la décima es imposible. ¡Es peor con los pasteles!

Unit 7: Adjective Pronouns

ejercicio I-7-1

1. Él compra coches nuevos, pero yo siempre compro los usados.
2. Ella prefiere los hombres altos, pero yo prefiero los bajos.
3. Ellos quieren la pregunta fácil, pero nosotros queremos la difícil.
4. Ella cree que el hombre rubio es guapo, pero yo prefiero el moreno.
5. La pluma azul es tuya, pero la verde es mía.
6. Cada cliente quiere comprar un coche de lujo, pero compra el compacto.
7. Más personas compran la alfombra gris porque la blanca siempre está sucia.
8. Los dos vestidos son hermosos, pero el largo es más elegante.
9. Él pone las lámparas grandes en la sala y las pequeñas en el dormitorio.
10. La copa grande es para el vino rojo, y la pequeña es para el blanco.

ejercicio I-7-2

1. Algunas personas viven en la ciudad y algunas viven en el campo.
2. El setenta por ciento de los dentistas usan este cepillo de dientes y los demás usan un palo.
3. No puedo decidir cuál es el mejor lavaplatos. Me gustan los dos (ambos).
4. Nunca voy de compras con ella. Compra todo. Es peligroso.
5. A Diego le gustan las fiestas. Siempre es el último en salir.
6. Mi esposo bebe (toma) leche todo el tiempo. Por eso, compro mucha cada semana.
7. Tengo varios libros de español. ¿Quieres uno?
8. A Esmeralda le encantan los zapatos. Tiene muchos.
9. En las reuniones, unas cuantas personas hablan todo el tiempo y la mayoría sufre en silencio.
10. Marcia recibe todos los regalos y pobrecita Jan no recibe ninguno.
11. Tenemos mucha ensalada. ¿Quieres más?
12. Usualmente, miles de personas vienen a la ceremonia, pero este año hay obviamente menos.
13. Los estudiantes van de excursión. Cada uno tiene una mochila.
14. Cada chica tiene un lápiz, pero varias no tienen papel.
15. Voy a pedir otro batido. ¿Quieres otro también?

ejercicio I-7-3

1. A menudo el menor lleva la ropa usada.
2. Todos creen que esto es brillante.
3. Nadie va a comer esto. ¡Está mohoso!
4. Alguien está en la cocina con Dinah.
5. Nuestra cliente favorita es la que gasta todo su dinero en los cosméticos y la ropa.
6. En *The Waltons*, John Boy es el mayor y Erin es la menor.
7. Para estos puestos, los que quieren trabajar diez horas al día pueden pedir una entrevista.
8. Muchos psicólogos estudian las diferencias entre el mayor y el menor en la familia.
9. Oscar Wilde escribe que un cínico es el que sabe el precio de todo y el valor de nada.
10. Todos sufren de vez en cuando, y la mayoría son más fuertes por la experiencia.
11. Todos están aquí, pero algunos no conocen a nadie.
12. Juan y Mateo viven juntos, pero ninguno tiene un televisor.
13. Cualquiera puede llevar estos pantalones.
14. Ramón da consejos a cualquiera.
15. Hay una fiesta esta noche. Cualesquiera de ustedes (vosotros) pueden ir conmigo.

ejercicio   I-7-4

1. ¿Tienes algo para mí?
2. De todas las cosas en el mundo, lo mejor es el amor.
3. No importa si yo llevo blue-jeans. Ella siempre lleva lo mismo.
4. A: ¿Cuál quieren ellos? B: Cualquiera. No importa.
5. Es maravilloso cuando ustedes bailan. Lo mejor es cuando bailan el mambo.
6. El servicio y el ambiente aquí son terribles. Pero lo peor es la comida.
7. Él nunca trae nada a una fiesta, pero siempre come y bebe todo.
8. Lo peor en una relación es no poder tener confianza en la otra persona.
9. Algunas personas creen que él es muy sabio, pero la verdad es que siempre dice lo mismo.
10. No sé nada acerca de esto.
11. Cualquiera de estos coches es bueno para el invierno.
12. Estos libros son interesantes. Puedes leer cualquiera de ellos.
13. Cualquiera de estos tres está bien.
14. Cualesquiera de estos están bien.

traducción   I-7-5

Este letrero dice: "Hoy es el primer día del resto de la vida". Si esto es verdad, entonces, ¿qué es mañana? ¿El segundo? No puedo creer todo lo que leo. Nadie puede. Algunos creen todo. Algunas personas creen los anuncios en las contraportadas de las revistas. Supongo que algunos de estos son la verdad, pero la mayoría de estos anuncios son mentiras. ¿Quiénes son estas personas no honradas? Prometen todo y no entregan nada.

Unit 8: Relative Pronouns

ejercicio   I-8-1

1. Tengo el libro que quieres.
2. Las personas que trabajan aquí son muy amables.
3. El coche que quiero es rojo.
4. Sólo miro películas que son de Europa.
5. Él cree que esta salsa está muy picante.
6. La medicina que tomo cada mañana sabe a gasolina.
7. Tienes dos libros que son buenos y dos que son malos.
8. La pintura que ves es por (de) Francisco Goya.
9. Él no sabe que yo tengo su billetera.
10. ¿Sabes que la mantequilla es pura grasa?
11. El hombre que vive en esta casa es actor.
12. Ella siempre alquila las películas que recomiendo.
13. Ella es la vieja que vive en un zapato.
14. Los gatos que tienen muchos dedos viven en Key West, Florida.
15. Las personas que votan tienen mucho poder.

ejercicio I-8-2

1. Su esposa, la cual (la que) es linda, habla cuatro idiomas.
2. Su perro, el cual (el que) es un perro de lana, ladra todo el tiempo.
3. Nuestra casa, la cual (la que) tiene cien años, es conocida por los fantasmas que viven en el desván.
4. Mis anillos, los cuales (los que) son de plata, son de Taxco, México.
5. Nuestros libros, los cuales (los que) todavía están en cajas, son muy valiosos.
6. El casero, el cual (el que) también vive en este edificio, es un hombre muy extraño.
7. Los niños (hijos) de mi vecino, los cuales (los que) son más ruidosos que un aeropuerto, son angelitos en la iglesia.
8. La poeta, la cual (la que) es la madre de dos hijas, escribe todos los días a la medianoche.
9. La Casa Blanca, la cual (la que) es popular con los turistas, es el hogar del Presidente de los Estados Unidos.
10. Estos vinos, los cuales (los que) son de Francia, tienen noventa años.
11. El párrafo, el cual (el que) acabo de leer, no tiene sentido.
12. Esta actitud de indiferencia, la cual (la que) no puedo tolerar, es contagiosa.

ejercicio I-8-3

1. Kitty es la mujer con quien vivo.
2. ¿Quién es el hombre con quien vives?
3. Éstas son las personas para quienes él trabaja.
4. El hombre a la izquierda es la persona con quien salgo.
5. Margo es la mujer para quien trabajo.
6. Francisco es el hombre en quien pienso.
7. Raúl es el chico con quien estoy enojado/a.
8. Bárbara es la persona por quien tengo compasión.
9. Ana es la mujer a quien veo.
10. Esos hombres son los jugadores a quienes miro.

ejercicio I-8-4

1. Él nunca recuerda lo que (yo) quiero.
2. Ella siempre come lo que (yo) como.
3. En tu cumpleaños, puedes pedir lo que quieras.
4. Lo que él dice siempre es mentira.
5. ¿Oyes (tú) lo que (yo) oigo? ¿Sabes (tú) lo que (yo) sé?
6. No comprende lo que lee.
7. Algunas personas siempre hacen lo que no deben hacer.
8. ¿Sabes lo que quieres hacer este fin de semana?
9. Ella come exactamente lo que es malo para ella.
10. Lo que (tú) necesitas es un abrazo.

ejercicio I-8-5

1. Marcos, cuya madre es dentista, quiere vender dulces.
2. El chico, cuyo libro tienes, es mi primo.
3. El actor, cuyas películas son terribles, es muy rico.
4. El dentista, cuyo consultorio está en la ciudad, vive en las afueras.
5. Los niños, cuyos padres hablan sólo inglés, estudian español.
6. Él es el hombre cuyo perro siempre roba nuestro periódico.
7. ¿Es usted la mujer cuyo árbol es tan hermoso?
8. ¿Son ellos los niños cuyo padre es el senador de Colorado?
9. El estudiante, cuya maestra es de Ecuador, quiere ir a Quito este verano.
10. La vieja señora Hubbard, cuyos gabinetes están vacíos, quiere dar un hueso a su perro.
11. Mark, cuyo padre es presidente de un banco, no puede sumar.
12. Lilia, cuya tienda es muy popular, es mi mejor amiga.

ejercicio I-8-6

1. que	5. a quien	9. que	13. a quien
2. lo que	6. con quienes	10. lo que	14. lo que
3. que	7. cuya	11. lo que	15. cuyo
4. cuyo	8. Lo que	12. que	

traducción I-8-7

Cabo San Lucas, que (el cual/el que) está en la punta sureña de Baja California, es un lugar maravilloso para vacaciones tranquilas. El área, que (la cual/la que) es principalmente un desierto, tiene muchos resortes elegantes que (los cuales/los que) tienen piscinas, restaurantes, bares, tiendas y clubes. En su mayor parte, usted puede hacer lo que quiera en la soledad de su habitación. Hay un centro, que (el cual/el que) es algo pequeño, que tiene una marina, que (la cual/la que) tiene muchos barcos para la pesca. Los turistas que quieren ir de pesca pueden alquilar un barco con un guía. Cualquier persona cuya idea de diversión es (el) calor y (el) sol puede estar muy contenta por (durante) una semana en Cabo San Lucas.

Unit 9: Direct Object Pronouns

ejercicio I-9-1

1. lo	4. la	7. la	10. lo	13. los
2. la	5. la	8. los	11. lo	14. las
3. los	6. los	9. lo	12. la	15. la

ejercicio I-9-2

1. Te amo. (Te quiero.)
2. Lo amo. (Lo quiero.)
3. Él me ama. (Él me quiere.)
4. Te veo.
5. Lo conozco. (La conozco.)
6. Ella lo ve.
7. Lo bebo.
8. La tengo.
9. Lo tienes.
10. Ella los tiene.
11. Me amas. (Me quieres.)
12. La amo. (La quiero.)
13. Ellos nos aman. (Ellos nos quieren.)
14. Me ves.
15. Me conocéis.
16. La vemos.
17. La comen.
18. Lo quiero.
19. La queremos.
20. Las tenemos.

ejercicio I-9-3

1. La compro en (*answer will vary*).
2. Los compro en (*answer will vary*).
3. Lo estudio en (*answer will vary*).
4. Sí, lo conozco.
5. Sí, lo tomo.
6. Sí la comprendo.
7. Sí, la leo.
8. Sí, lo leo.
9. Sí, la hago.
10. Sí, la conozco.
11. Sí, las veo.
12. Sí, lo como.
13. Sí, las miro.
14. Sí, los leo.

ejercicio I-9-4

1. No lo tengo.
2. Ella no la ve.
3. No lo conozco.
4. No me conoces.
5. Ellos no la compran.
6. Él no lo escribe.
7. Ellos no los leen.
8. Ella no lo gana.
9. No lo llevo.
10. No te vemos.

11. No la tienes.
12. Ellos no lo ven.
13. Él no me conoce.
14. Ellos no nos conocen.
15. No lo usamos.
16. Ella no lo lee.
17. No las cantamos.
18. Ustedes no lo tienen.
19. Nunca (Jamás) los llevas.
20. Nunca (Jamás) nos ves.

ejercicio I-9-5

1. lavarla
2. comerla
3. escribirlo
4. limpiarla
5. tocarlas
6. bailarlo
7. construirlos
8. verlo
9. conocerla
10. oírla
11. verlo
12. prepararlas
13. oírla
14. conocerlos
15. visitarlo

ejercicio I-9-6

1. Él me quiere ver.
2. Ella lo quiere besar.
3. Los debes comer.
4. Ellos lo tienen que hacer.
5. Las queremos conocer.
6. Ella tiene que cantarla.
7. Debo leerlo.
8. Quiero verte mañana.
9. Ellos necesitan tenerlo para mañana.
10. Juan puede vernos.

ejercicio I-9-7

1. ¿Quieres verla conmigo?
2. ¿Vas a comerlo?
3. ¿Debemos beberla ahora o debemos ponerla en el refrigerador?
4. ¿Podemos comerlo o debemos tirarlo a la basura?
5. No debes ponerlos en la sala.
6. Si no quieres tenerla, debes ponerla en la caja y devolverla.
7. No puedo llevarlos a una fiesta formal.
8. ¿Por qué no puedes verme?
9. No tienes que hacerlo hoy.
10. ¿Quieres abrirlas en la mañana y cerrarlas en la noche?

ejercicio I-9-8

1. No los quiero ver esta noche.
2. No la debes devolver.
3. ¿Por qué no lo puedes decir?
4. No la vamos a ver en la biblioteca.
5. No las puede tirar a la basura.
6. ¿Cuándo las puedo ver?
7. Si no lo quieres oír, puedes apagar la radio.
8. ¿Dónde los quieres guardar? ¿Los podemos poner aquí?
9. ¿La van a vender (ustedes)?
10. ¡No, no lo puedes golpear!

traducción   I-9-9

Yo sé que Marcos tiene mi dinero, mis zapatos, y la mesa y las sillas para mi comedor. Él cree que no sé esto, pero sí, lo sé. Primero, el dinero. Sé que lo tiene porque puedo verlo (lo puedo ver) en aquella gaveta. Segundo, los zapatos. Los necesito porque si no los llevo, no puedo correr rápido ni saltar bien. Tercero, la mesa. No sé por qué la tiene ni por qué la quiere. Quiero ponerla (La quiero poner) en mi nueva casa. Él cree que las sillas son suyas, pero no es verdad. Son mías. Y las quiero ahora.

Unit 10: Indirect Object Pronouns

ejercicio   I-10-1

Direct Object	**Indirect Object**
1. a story	me
2. nothing	him
3. food	us
4. meal	us
5. us	friends
6. it (understood)	you
7. ring	you
8. drinks	everyone
9. letter (note, etc.)	me
10. diamonds	her

ejercicio   I-10-2

1. me
2. nos
3. le
4. Les
5. le
6. Le
7. Le
8. Le
9. Me
10. nos
11. les
12. Os
13. Les
14. te
15. le

ejercicio   I-10-3

1. Le digo la verdad.
2. Él me dice mentiras todo el tiempo.
3. Le damos las flores.
4. Les escribo una carta cada semana.
5. Ellos nos escriben cada mes.
6. Ella le canta una canción.
7. John es mi ayudante y le dicto una carta.
8. Siempre le digo que es bonita.
9. Les envío (mando) una tarjeta para su aniversario.
10. ¿Qué te dan para tu cumpleaños cada año?

ejercicio   I-10-4

1. Él no me dice nada.
2. Yo no le digo nada.
3. Ellos nunca le envían nada porque no saben su dirección.
4. No le doy dinero.
5. El mesero (El camarero) no te canta "Feliz cumpleaños".
6. ¿Por qué no le dicen la verdad?
7. ¿Por qué no os compran una computadora?
8. Les sirvo la cena, pero nunca me dan las gracias.
9. Si no me hacen preguntas, no les digo mentiras.
10. No les prestamos dinero.

ejercicio I-10-5

1. darle
2. decirles
3. prestarme
4. alquilarles
5. decirte

6. escribirle
7. cantaros
8. decirnos
9. mostrarle
10. contarnos

11. diseñarme
12. prepararles
13. decirles
14. venderles
15. servirnos

ejercicio I-10-6

1. Le quiero dar un regalo.
2. Él me necesita decir la verdad.
3. Le debemos escribir una carta.
4. Nos debes escribir más a menudo.
5. Les tienen que decir la verdad.
6. Debemos darles aceite de oliva.
7. Él quiere comprarle un diamante.
8. Cuando él viene a nuestra casa, siempre quiere traernos algo.
9. Puedo enviarte (mandarte) estos floreros por correo.
10. Necesitáis decirle algo.

ejercicio I-10-7

1. ¿Quieres traerme un gatito? / ¿Me quieres traer un gatito?
2. No vamos a mostrarles nuestra casa nueva. / No les vamos a mostrar nuestra casa nueva.
3. ¿Quieres venderles estas pinturas? / ¿Les quieres vender estas pinturas?
4. ¿Quién va a pagarme el dinero? / ¿Quién me va a pagar el dinero?
5. ¿Puedes enviarnos los muebles para el martes? / ¿Nos puedes enviar los muebles para el martes?
6. El artista no puede pintarle un cuadro para junio. / El artista no le puede pintar un cuadro para junio.
7. No voy a lavarte la ropa. / No te voy a lavar la ropa.
8. No queremos decirles (contarles) las malas noticias. / No les queremos decir (contar) las malas noticias.
9. ¿Cuándo podéis construirnos el edificio? / ¿Cuándo nos podéis construir el edificio?
10. ¿Debes leerle tal carta? / ¿Le debes leer tal carta?

ejercicio I-10-8

1. Le digo a Juan todo.
2. Quiero decirle (Le quiero decir) todo a él.
3. Ella le escribe a su tía cada mes.
4. ¿Por qué le traes tanto a Mateo?
5. Ella le da los documentos a su abogado.
6. Ella tiene que darle (le tiene que dar) el dinero a la policía.
7. ¡Margarita nos regala a nosotros un televisor!
8. ¡Oliver quiere regalarme (me quiere regalar) a mí un reloj de Cartier!
9. A: ¿Qué les haces a tus amigos? B: Les hago una torta.
10. Les traigo a ellos un periódico cada mañana.
11. Usualmente les compro a ellas ropa para Navidad.
12. ¿Qué debemos comprarle (le debemos comprar) a ella?
13. Romeo le envía (manda) rosas a Julieta en el día de San Valentín.
14. ¿Van a enviarles (mandarles) algo a ustedes este año? (¿Les van a enviar [mandar] algo a ustedes este año?)
15. George Washington no puede decirle (le puede decir) una mentira a nadie.

ejercicio   I-10-9

1. Sí, me gusta la leche. / No, no me gusta la leche.
2. Sí, me gustan los dramas de Shakespeare. / No, no me gustan los dramas de Shakespeare.
3. Sí, me gusta comer en el coche. / No, no me gusta comer en el coche.
4. Sí, me gusta limpiar la casa. / No, no me gusta limpiar la casa.
5. Sí, me gustan los platos exóticos. / No, no me gustan los platos exóticos.
6. Sí, me gustan las películas de horror. / No, no me gustan las películas de horror.
7. Sí, me gusta correr. / No, no me gusta correr.
8. Sí, me gusta memorizar los verbos españoles. / No, no me gusta memorizar los verbos españoles.
9. Sí, me gustan los mosquitos. / No, no me gustan los mosquitos.
10. Sí, me gusta conducir en la hora punta. / No, no me gusta conducir en la hora punta.

ejercicio   I-10-10

1. Me fascina este libro.
2. No quiero nada más. Me basta esta comida. (Esta comida me basta.)
3. A Mikey le gusta todo.
4. Me disgusta esta película. (Esta película me disgusta.)
5. Me duelen los ojos.
6. A él no le importa nada (nada le importa) y no le interesa nada (nada le interesa). ¡Qué triste!
7. Me falta un botón en mi camisa.
8. ¡Nos encanta tu nueva casa!
9. ¿Qué te molesta?
10. Estas revistas me parecen absurdas.
11. Después de los días de fiesta, a ellos no les sobra dinero.
12. A él le disgusta el café, pero a mí me encanta.
13. Me vuelve loco/a (encanta) esta obra de teatro.
14. No me caen bien las galletas con pasas.
15. A ella le encantan los deportes, pero a él le disgustan.

traducción   I-10-11

Tengo un nuevo vecino. Él vive al lado de mí. Él me parece muy amable. Quiero regalarle (a él) algo que le gusta. Puedo hacerle una torta o puedo escribirle una nota que dice, "¡Bienvenido al vecindario!" Puedo verlo ahora. ¡Estos prismáticos son fantásticos! Puedo verlo todo ahora. Pienso (Creo) que voy a mirarlo por un rato. Nadie me ve cuando uso mis prismáticos porque apago todas las luces. Me encantan estos prismáticos. No sé lo que debo hacer. Voy a preguntarle a mi tía lo que piensa. Ella siempre me da buenos consejos.

Unit 11: Reflexive Object Pronouns

ejercicio   I-11-1

1. Me ducho.
2. Me baño.
3. Te duchas cada día.
4. Él se afeita cada mañana.
5. Ella se cepilla los dientes tres veces al día.
6. Nos cepillamos los dientes.
7. Ellos se afeitan dos veces al día.
8. Él se lava el pelo.
9. Me lavo la cara.
10. Te secas el pelo.
11. Usted se seca con una toalla.
12. Me peino (el pelo) a menudo.
13. Ella se peina (el pelo) casi nunca.
14. Me peso en la báscula de baño.
15. Ella se pesa dos veces al día.

ejercicio **I-11-2**

1. Cuando me pruebo ropa nueva, me veo (me miro) en el espejo.
2. ¿A qué hora te acuestas y a qué hora te levantas?
3. Normalmente las personas se casan durante los fines de semana.
4. Me enfermo (Me pongo enfermo/a) cuando como comida que tiene mucha grasa.
5. Me voy al trabajo cada mañana a las ocho.
6. Me ducho, me cepillo los dientes, me seco el pelo, me visto y después me voy al trabajo.
7. Me pongo enfermo/a cuando veo un pelo en la comida.
8. Miss América se desmaya cuando se pone la corona.
9. Cada noche me desvisto, me pongo el pijama, me acuesto y me duermo.
10. Cuando Laura se queda en un hotel, se preocupa por la seguridad de su familia.

ejercicio **I-11-3**

1. me	4. me	7. se	10. os
2. se	5. se	8. me	11. me
3. nos	6. se	9. te	12. se, se

ejercicio **I-11-4**

1. Después de vestirme, me miro en el espejo.
2. Antes de irnos, nos ponemos los abrigos, las manoplas y los sombreros.
3. Después de bañarme, me pongo la bata y me relajo.
4. En vez de ducharme, voy a bañarme esta noche.
5. Este jabón es el mejor para lavarse la cara.
6. Uso este champú para lavarme el pelo.
7. Cuando me quedo en un hotel, siempre pido una llamada para despertarme.
8. Él toma una pastilla cada noche para dormirse.
9. Algunas personas meditan para relajarse.
10. Necesitáis una navaja y una hoja para afeitaros.

ejercicio **I-11-5**

1. Para nuestra luna de miel, queremos quedarnos en un hotel elegante.
2. ¿Dónde van a quedarse en París?
3. Tengo mucho calor. Voy a quitarme el suéter.
4. Tengo mucho frío. Tengo que ponerme el abrigo.
5. Nadie quiere enfermarse, pero desgraciadamente esto ocurre.
6. A nuestro perro le gusta bañarse en la piscina de nuestros vecinos.
7. Si quieres lavarte el pelo, hay champú en el gabinete.
8. Si quiere afeitarse, el conserje puede darle una navaja y algunas hojas.
9. Si quieren ponerse bien, tienen que tomar este caldo de pollo.
10. Vas a enfermarte si comes esa carne cruda.

traducción **I-11-6**

"¡Él ya no se baña nunca! Es absolutamente terrible." Mi vecina me dice todo, y hoy ella se queja de su esposo. Es una mujer fastidiosa y se queja todo el tiempo. Me dice que debo lavarme el pelo más a menudo. Le digo que eso es mi problema y que ella debe callarse. Me dice que no puede callarse cuando nadie en su familia ni se baña ni se ducha. Me dice que después de acostarse, no puede dormirse porque se preocupa por todas estas personas que no se lavan. Yo le digo que (ella) puede comprarse o un bote de Lysol o una manguera.

Unit 12: RID: Sentences with Two Object Pronouns

ejercicio **I-12-1**

1. Él me lo da.
2. Ella te lo dice.
3. Te lo damos.
4. Te la escribo.
5. Él nos los envía.
6. Te la cantamos.
7. ¿Por qué me lo das?
8. ¿Quién te lo tiene?
9. ¿Cuándo me lo haces?
10. ¿Por qué nos lo dices?
11. Me la preparo.
12. (Ella) Se las compra.

ejercicio **I-12-2**

1. Él se la canta.
2. Se lo decimos.
3. Se los compras.
4. Se lo escribo.
5. Se los envía.
6. Se lo digo.
7. Se la vende.
8. Se las das.
9. Nadie se lo dice.
10. ¿Por qué se lo dices?
11. Se las traemos.
12. Ella se lo cocina.
13. Se las hago.
14. ¿Se los haces?
15. ¿Quién se lo da?

ejercicio **I-12-3**

1. Ella no me lo dice.
2. No se lo digo.
3. No nos las compramos.
4. Ellos no nos la envían a tiempo.
5. Ella no nos lo hace cada día.
6. No se la doy.
7. Él no me lo paga en efectivo.
8. Él no me lo da a tiempo.
9. ¿Por qué no se la envías mañana?
10. ¿Se las compras cada día?
11. Nunca me las compro.
12. Nunca se los decimos.

ejercicio **I-12-4**

1. Quiero decírtelo. / Te lo quiero decir.
2. Quiero comprártela. / Te la quiero comprar.
3. Tienes que dármelo. / Me lo tienes que dar.
4. Tenemos que vendértelos. / Te los tenemos que vender.
5. Tenemos que vendérselo. / Se lo tenemos que vender.
6. Ellos deben comprártelas. / Ellos te las deben comprar.
7. Ellos deben comprárselo. / Ellos se lo deben comprar.
8. Ella necesita enviármela. / Ella me la necesita enviar.
9. (Ustedes) Tienen que dárnosla. / (Ustedes) Nos la tienen que dar.
10. Debo traérselo. / Se lo debo traer.

11. Ellos deben traérmelas. / Ellos me las deben traer.
12. Ella quiere cantárnosla. / Ella nos la quiere cantar.
13. Puedes enviármelo por correo. / Me lo puedes enviar por correo.
14. Él puede pagártela en efectivo. / Él te la puede pagar en efectivo.
15. Quiero pagároslos con un cheque. / Os los quiero pagar con un cheque.

ejercicio   I-12-5

1. ¿Puedes hacérmelo? / ¿Me lo puedes hacer?
2. No, no puedo hacértelo. / No, no te lo puedo hacer.
3. ¿Tenemos que decírsela? / ¿Se la tenemos que decir?
4. ¿Cuándo quieres dárselas? / ¿Cuándo se las quieres dar?
5. No necesitas pagármelo ahora. / No me lo necesitas pagar ahora.
6. Ellos no pueden vendértelo en los Estados Unidos. / Ellos no te lo pueden vender en los Estados Unidos.
7. No podemos vendérsela a este precio. / No se la podemos vender a este precio.
8. ¿Cuándo quieres decírmelo? / ¿Cuándo me lo quieres decir?
9. ¿No vas a traérnoslo hoy? / ¿No nos lo vas a traer hoy?
10. ¿No pueden enviárnoslas por correo? / ¿No nos las pueden enviar por correo?

traducción   I-12-6

Cada año recibo muchos regalos para mi cumpleaños. Tengo muchos amigos que tienen tiendas y (ellos) siempre me regalan lo que venden o lo que hacen. Y para sus cumpleaños yo les doy regalos también. Mi amigo Merlin vende flores, y me las regala. Manolo vende zapatos y me los regala (da). Juan vende café y me lo regala (da). Vidal vende champú y me lo regala (da). Paloma hace perfume y me lo envía (manda) porque vive en España. Donna hace vestidos y me los envía (manda). Elsa hace joyas y siempre me hace algo para mi cumpleaños. Este año quiero un avión privado. ¿Quién va a regalármelo? (¿Quién me lo va a regalar?)

Unit 13: Reciprocal Pronouns

ejercicio   I-13-1

1. Nos / We know each other very well.
2. se / They love each other a lot.
3. Os / You see each other through the window.
4. Se / Do you know each other?
5. Se / They (You) kiss each other every morning.
6. nos / Every day we tell each other "I love you."
7. se / When they are angry, they don't speak (talk) to each other.
8. Os / Do you visit each other often?
9. se, se / They fight (with each other) a lot because they hate each other.
10. Nos / We speak (talk) to each other on the telephone three times every week.
11. se / They want to know each other better.
12. nos / We can't see each other as often as we want.

ejercicio I-13-2

1. Nos escribimos cartas largas cada semana.
2. ¿Cuándo os veis?
3. ¿Por qué se gritan tanto?
4. Los tórtolos se cantan en la copa del árbol.
5. Nos compramos regalos cada diciembre.
6. Se encuentran en el gimnasio cada viernes por la tarde.
7. No podemos hablarnos porque mi teléfono no funciona.
8. No deben decirse todo. Él no puede guardar un secreto.
9. Podéis miraros ahora.
10. Mis vecinos se gritan cada sábado por la noche.

traducción I-13-3

Voy a la reunión de mi escuela secundaria en dos semanas. Estoy muy ilusionada porque Enrique va a asistir. Yo sé esto porque mi mejor amiga, Laura, es la secretaria de la clase. Ella y yo nos hablamos cada semana y (ella) me dice (cuenta) todo. Estas reuniones son delicadas. Queremos vernos, pero al mismo tiempo no queremos vernos. O, tal vez, queremos vernos en el pasado, lo cual ya no existe. Algunas personas se ven después de muchos años y es maravilloso. Pero hay otras personas que se ven y no es maravilloso.

Unit 14: *Se* and the Passive Voice

ejercicio I-14-1

1. vende
2. come
3. hacen
4. bailan
5. cultivan
6. exportan
7. baila
8. fabrican
9. liman
10. fabrica

ejercicio I-14-2

Syntax may vary.
1. Se habla español aquí.
2. Se hablan español y francés aquí.
3. Se venden zapatos allí.
4. No se venden fuegos artificiales a los adolescentes. (Los fuegos artificiales no se venden a los adolescentes.)
5. No se permite la entrada antes de las diez. (La entrada no se permite antes de las diez.)
6. No se permiten las cámaras en el teatro. (Las cámaras no se permiten en el teatro.)
7. El oro y las joyas no se consideran buenas inversiones.
8. Las tiendas y los museos se cierran los martes.
9. El banco se cierra a las dos y media.
10. Se fabrican piñatas en esta fábrica.

ejercicio I-14-3

Syntax may vary.
1. Se debe pagar los impuestos cada abril.
2. No se puede estar en dos lugares al mismo tiempo.
3. Se necesita cambiar el aceite en el coche cada tres mil millas.

4. No se debe culpar a los otros (a los demás) por los resultados de sus acciones.
5. Se debe hacer ejercicio y meditar diariamente.
6. Se debe hacer más claros estos mapas. ¡No se puede leer esto!
7. No se puede extraer la sangre de un nabo.
8. No se puede juzgar un libro por su portada.
9. Se debe cepillar los dientes después de comer.
10. Se puede nadar y jugar al tenis en este club.
11. Para bailar La Bamba, se necesita una poca de gracia.
12. Nunca se explicaron los OVNIs.
13. ¿Se puede entrar?
14. En esta tienda se paga un precio fijo.
15. Se dice que se debe mirar antes de saltar.

ejercicio   I-14-4

1. El centro comercial se cierra a las nueve y media.
2. Me enojo (Me pongo enojado/a) cuando pago siete dólares para ver una película y el proyector se descompone.
3. Usualmente, las bombillas se queman después de cien horas.
4. Cuando se estropea un coche en la autopista, es un catástrofe para todos.
5. ¿A qué hora se abre ese restaurante?
6. El sol se pone a las ocho y media de la noche en el verano.
7. Con este aparato, las luces se encienden y se apagan automáticamente.
8. Después de los días de fiesta, se rompen millones de juguetes.
9. Cuando ella canta, se quiebran todos los vasos.
10. Los museos se cierran a las seis en punto.

traducción   I-14-5

Quiero ir a Madrid para mis próximas vacaciones. Tengo un folleto conmigo ahora. ¡A ver! ¿Qué se puede hacer en Madrid? Se dice aquí que el Prado es uno de los mejores museos del mundo y que se puede pasar varios días explorando sus tesoros. Se dice que en Madrid el sistema del metro es muy bueno, así que no se necesita alquilar un coche. Se puede tomar el metro a todos los sitios en la ciudad. Si se va a un buen restaurante en Madrid, se puede probar el cochinillo asado. También, El Retiro es un parque precioso y se puede alquilar barquitos para recorrer el estanque. Se puede asistir a las corridas y se puede bailar hasta las cinco de la mañana. ¡Se puede hacer de todo en esta ciudad maravillosa!

PART II   Prepositions

Unit 1: Prepositions (and Related Terms)

ejercicio   II-1-1

1. Él siempre habla acerca de su novia.
2. Prefiero el café con leche y azúcar.
3. Él prefiere el té sin azúcar.
4. *Don Quijote* es la mejor novela del mundo, según José.
5. Además de flores, su novio le da dulces en cada cita.

6. La espalda del director está contra la pared.
7. Este libro es sobre George Washington.
8. Ellos no escriben mucho acerca de sus problemas.
9. ¿Quieres la pizza con carne o sin carne?
10. Me gusta todo aquí excepto (salvo; menos) los zapatos.
11. Su tesis es sobre el arte de Roma.
12. Según Julia, sus amigos no saben nada acerca de la música clásica.
13. Quiero todo contra la pared, menos (salvo; excepto) el podio.
14. Tienes que servir las bebidas además de la comida.
15. La biblioteca no tiene nada sobre la historia de la pizza.

ejercicio   II-1-2

1. Hay un libro encima de la mesa.
2. Juan está a la derecha de mí y Felipe está a la izquierda.
3. ¿Vives al lado de nuestro restaurante?
4. Cada primavera sembramos flores delante de la casa.
5. Necesitamos más iluminación sobre los cuadros.
6. La gente a través del país miran los juegos olímpicos en la televisión.
7. Mi canción favorita es "Cerca de ti".
8. Muchas personas quieren (Mucha gente quiere) vivir lejos del aeropuerto.
9. ¿Sabes que hay un tigre debajo de tu cama?
10. ¿Por qué hay tantos perros fuera de tu casa?
11. ¿Quién está en la cocina con Dinah?
12. ¿Qué tienes dentro de la boca?
13. Él trabaja en el banco.
14. Ellos están en el banco.
15. No hay nada en la televisión esta noche.
16. No hay nada entre nosotros.
17. ¿Quién está detrás de ti?
18. La obra es en el teatro.

ejercicio   II-1-3

1. a lo largo de
2. más allá de
3. alrededor de
4. por
5. hacia
6. hacia adelante
7. a lo largo de
8. hacia
9. por
10. más allá de
11. hacia atrás
12. alrededor de

ejercicio   II-1-4

1. Corro alrededor del lago cada mañana.
2. ¿Caminas (Andas) a lo largo del bulevar?
3. El detective busca por la casa.
4. Él siempre mira hacia sus metas.
5. Superman puede volar por el aire.
6. Cada noche, caminan (andan) por el centro comercial.
7. Si miras más allá de ese árbol, puedes ver la montaña rusa.
8. ¿Quieres caminar (andar) alrededor de la cuadra conmigo?
9. No puedes ir más allá del final de esta cuadra.
10. Podemos conducir hacia el río y después caminar (andar) a lo largo de la senda.
11. Nancy Kerrigan puede patinar hacia adelante y hacia atrás.
12. Superman puede volar, pero no vuela hacia atrás.

ejercicio II-1-5

1. Iowa está al norte de Missouri.
2. Arkansas está al sur de Missouri.
3. Kansas está al oeste de Missouri.
4. Illinois está al este de Missouri.
5. Michigan está al nordeste de Missouri.
6. Nebraska está al noroeste de Missouri.
7. Oklahoma está al suroeste (sudoeste) de Missouri.
8. Tennessee está al sureste (sudeste) de Missouri.
9. Louisiana está al sur de Missouri.
10. Minnesota está al norte de Missouri.

ejercicio II-1-6

1. A causa de (Por) este resfriado, no puedo ir al cine con mis amigos.
2. Leo (Estoy leyendo) un libro de John Steinbeck.
3. Este libro es para ustedes.
4. ¡Saludos desde Cancún!
5. Vamos al centro comercial. ¿Quieres ir con nosotros?
6. Estas perlas son de Japón.
7. Todos mis amigos de la universidad están aquí.
8. ¿Qué quieren de mí?
9. No tengo nada para ti.
10. Él me llama desde Alemania cada semana.
11. Por (A causa de) su actitud y amargura, ella no tiene amigos.
12. La novela *Sophie's Choice* es de William Styron.
13. Marchamos (Estamos marchando) a Pretoria.
14. ¡Uno de ellos va a ganar el premio gordo!
15. Estoy cansado/a, y por esta razón voy a dormir una siesta.

ejercicio II-1-7

1. después de
2. durante
3. hasta
4. Antes de
5. desde
6. a
7. después de
8. durante
9. antes de
10. durante
11. después
12. por

ejercicio II-1-8

1. No tienes que estar aquí hasta mañana.
2. Necesito limpiar el garaje antes del invierno.
3. A: Hace frío, ¿no? B: Sí. Desde el martes.
4. Algunas personas creen que los fantasmas viven después de la muerte.
5. Después de la cena, siempre lavamos los platos.
6. ¿Qué quieres hacer durante nuestro descanso?
7. Usualmente, ¿qué haces por la tarde?
8. ¿Qué quieres hacer antes del baile?
9. Usualmente hablamos durante los anuncios.
10. Él va a trabajar aquí hasta marzo.
11. A: ¿No tienes leche? B: No. No desde el sábado.
12. Ellos trabajan de lunes a viernes.
13. Podemos mirar la película e ir al restaurante después.
14. Siempre pico las cebollas antes.

ejercicio II-1-9

1. abajo
2. arriba
3. adentro
4. afuera

5. arriba
6. adentro
7. afuera
8. abajo

9. adentro
10. afuera

ejercicio II-1-10

Answers will vary.

1. Mi dormitorio está adentro (arriba; abajo).
2. Mi coche está adentro (afuera).
3. Estoy adentro (arriba; abajo; afuera).
4. Los murciélagos duermen adentro (arriba).
5. El horno (de mi casa) está adentro (abajo).

6. Estoy adentro (abajo).
7. El baño principal (de mi casa) está arriba (abajo).
8. El tejado está arriba.
9. Los árboles más grandes están afuera.
10. Los árboles decorados para la Navidad están adentro.

Unit 2: *Para* and *Por*

ejercicio II-2-1

1. g
2. b
3. f
4. c
5. j

6. f
7. d
8. a
9. i
10. e

11. j
12. d
13. i
14. j
15. b

16. e
17. h
18. c
19. a
20. i

ejercicio II-2-2

1. Esta casa es perfecta para nosotros.
2. Necesitamos una mesa nueva para el comedor.
3. Para algunas personas, no es importante tener un coche.
4. Estos zapatos son para bailar el tango.
5. Tienes que leer este libro para el jueves.
6. Él mira la televisión para evitar sus problemas.
7. Salgo para África mañana.
8. Estudio para mago.

9. Él es muy cortés para un adolescente.
10. ¿Puedes escribir la carta para el martes?
11. Esta comida es para el gato.
12. Para él, el invierno es maravilloso, pero para mí, el verano es la mejor estación.
13. Ella trabaja mucho para sacar buenas notas.
14. ¿A qué hora sales para el trabajo?
15. Estas manzanas no son para comer.

ejercicio II-2-3

1. a
2. j
3. m
4. d
5. c

6. o
7. n
8. b
9. f
10. g

11. e
12. l
13. i
14. h
15. b

16. d
17. o
18. m
19. k
20. e

21. h
22. j
23. i
24. f
25. g

ejercicio II-2-4

1. Vamos a la escuela (al colegio) por autobús.
2. Puedes tener esos zapatos por diez dólares.
3. Él tiene por lo menos veinte gatos.
4. Cuando viajo, siempre camino por la ciudad e investigo todo.
5. Leemos el periódico por treinta minutos cada mañana.
6. Juanita está enferma hoy. ¿Puedes trabajar por ella?
7. Voy al supermercado por leche, mantequilla y huevos.
8. Cada lunes por la noche él mira (el) fútbol americano en la televisión.
9. Por sus alergias, no puede tocar el gato.
10. Gracias por nada.
11. Por dar tanto a los otros (a los demás), ella merece una medalla.
12. El noventa por ciento de todos los dentistas dicen que esta pasta de dientes es horrible.
13. Él viene por mi casa de vez en cuando.
14. Sólo tengo estimación por ti.
15. Ahora entiendo las diferencias entre *por* y *para* por primera vez.
16. Puedes enviarme los contratos por fax.

ejercicio II-2-5

1. para / recipient of an item or action
2. para / comparison to a certain standard
3. por / expresses thanks
4. por / duration of time
5. por / indicates motion, through, around
6. para / time limit of an action
7. para / recipient of an item or action
8. por, por, por / used before periods of the 24-hour day
9. para / destination
10. por, por / means of transportation
11. por / expresses exchange, price
12. para / expresses final destination
13. por / idiomatic expression
14. por / tells why something is a certain way
15. para / in order to do something
16. por / in behalf of
17. por / expresses per
18. por / idiomatic expression
19. para / expresses an opinion
20. por / shows point of temporary stop
21. por / shows emotion
22. para / in order to do something; for the purpose of
23. por / expresses "because of"
24. por / tells why something is a certain way
25. por / expresses means of information
26. por / idiomatic expression
27. para / in order to
28. por / used before periods in the 24-hour day
29. por / expresses per
30. para / time limit of an action

ejercicio II-2-6

Wording of explanations will vary.

1. A. You can have my shirt for your skirt. Destination: figuratively, "to go with"
   B. You can have my shirt for your skirt. Substitution: an equal exchange

2. A. We're going to their house tonight. Destination: The implication is that we will stay for a while.
   B. We're going by their house tonight. Movement: The implication is that their house is a temporary stop.

3. A. I have lots of shampoo and soap samples for the trip. Deadline: The trip is in the future.
   B. I have lots of shampoo and soap samples because of the trip. Motivation: "because of"

4. A. Martin and Dorothy have many toys for Daisy. Recipient of an action: The toys are *for* her.
   B. Martin and Dorothy have a lot of love for Daisy. Emotion: Tells of their feelings

5. A. Judith dances for Twyla. Destination: Twyla is the recipient of Judith's dancing.
   B. Judith dances for Twyla. Substitution: Judith is dancing on behalf of Twyla, who can't dance for some reason.

6. A. We're driving to the park. Destination: The park is our final destination.
   B. We're driving through/throughout the park. Movement: We're moving in/within an area.

7. A. These creams are for allergies. Destination: Allergies are a figurative destination.
   B. These allergies are because of the creams. Motivation: Tells why the allergies exist.

8. A. In my opinion, this soup is spoiled (bad). Standard: personal opinion
   B. Because of me this soup is spoiled (bad). Motivation: Tells why the soup has gone bad.

traducción   II-2-7

Ésta es una historia para todos. Hay una mujer que vive en Texas. Ella trabaja para una compañía grande, pero trabaja por muy poco dinero. Necesita más dinero para (la) comida y (la) ropa. Cada viernes por la tarde, cuando compra gasolina, paga dos dólares adicionales por billetes de la lotería. Ella escoge los números de la lotería por las edades de amigos y por fechas especiales. Esta semana, por primera vez, ella gana. Gana mil millones de dólares. Es suficiente dinero para comprar todo lo que quiere. Primero, ella compra regalos para todos sus amigos. Por supuesto, ellos le dicen: "Gracias por estos regalos". Normalmente, ella no paga más de cincuenta dólares por un vestido; sin embargo, por ganar la lotería, mañana va para París para comprar un vestido por cincuenta mil dólares. ¿Estás feliz por ella?

Unit 3: Verbs and Prepositions

ejercicio   II-3-1

1. Agradezco todo.
2. A: ¿Qué buscas? B: Busco mis anteojos.
3. ¿Dónde debemos colgar nuestros abrigos?
4. Me gusta escuchar la música clásica.
5. Puedes pagar la ropa en efectivo o con una tarjeta de crédito.
6. La niñera recoge los juguetes.
7. Él borra todos sus errores.
8. Esta noche Carlota va a salir con Guillermo. Está muy ilusionada.
9. Yo siempre saco la basura. Tú debes sacar la basura de vez en cuando.
10. El abogado entrega la evidencia al juez.
11. Los trapos empapan el aceite.
12. El cartero siempre pisa las rosas.
13. Necesito más dinero. Voy a pedir un aumento mañana.
14. ¿Por cuánto tiempo tenemos que esperar el autobús?
15. Puedes encender las luces aquí y apagar las luces allá.

ejercicio II-3-2

1. Vamos a conducir (manejar) a Vermont en vez de (en lugar de) volar.
2. Antes de comprar los huevos, debes mirar dentro del cartón.
3. Siempre me siento mejor después de hacer ejercicio.
4. Además de poder volar, Superman puede ver a través de las paredes.
5. Pienso en escribir una novela.
6. Para llegar al banco, debes doblar a la derecha en la avenida Park.
7. ¿Quieres nadar en vez de (en lugar de) jugar al golf?
8. Ella siempre come diez tacos después de nadar.
9. ¿Qué tienes que hacer antes de salir?
10. Voy a una conferencia sobre usar computadoras.
11. ¡Además de hervir el agua, esta estufa puede hervir la leche!
12. John tiene que tomar otras tres clases para graduarse.

ejercicio II-3-3

1. Esto suena a mentira.
2. Ella rompe a llorar cada vez que recuerda el dolor de su niñez.
3. Él va a renunciar a su trabajo porque su compañía va a empezar a recortar el personal.
4. Tarde o temprano, tienes que resignarte al hecho de que algunas personas no son honradas.
5. No puedes obligarnos a hacer nada que no queremos hacer.
6. Benjamín da cuerda a su reloj cada día a las nueve de la mañana.
7. La Sra. Golcalvo anima a sus hijos a estudiar bellas artes.
8. En esta casa nos sentamos a cenar a las siete en punto.
9. ¿A qué hora subimos al tren?
10. Es imposible forzar a Carmen a subir a la montaña rusa.
11. Mateo dice que la carne de culebra sabe a pollo.
12. Oscar Wilde dice que puede resistirse a todo salvo a la tentación.
13. En esta sección del libro, aprendemos a usar los verbos que toman la preposición *a*.
14. Algunos atletas se acostumbran a recibir y a gastar mucho dinero.
15. Ricardo no se dispone a darnos nada hoy. No está de humor.

ejercicio II-3-4

1. Puedes contar conmigo, pero, ¿puedo contar contigo?
2. Cada miércoles, me encuentro con Kay para cenar y (para) conversar.
3. En la película Superman, Clark Kent sale con Lois Lane.
4. Me asusto con la oscuridad durante una tormenta.
5. Es trágico, pero a veces una persona necesita romper con su familia.
6. El egoísta sueña con ser famoso, popular y rico.
7. No me asocio con compañías que venden tabaco.
8. De vez en cuando me equivoco con las personas.
9. Siempre nos divertimos con nuestros vecinos.
10. Ella se enfada (se enoja) conmigo cuando llego tarde.
11. José no se trata con la familia de su esposa.
12. Si limpias la bañera con Brillo, vas a dañarla.
13. De vez en cuando me doy con alguien que verdaderamente me inspira.
14. Si Juan no tiene cuidado, va a tropezarse con la pared.
15. Los domingos por la mañana, me contento a menudo con un jugo de naranja y el periódico.

ejercicio   II-3-5

1. Él siempre se olvida de tomar su medicina.
2. Este sofá sirve de una cama cómoda.
3. Tenemos que terminar de limpiar la casa para las cuatro y media.
4. Cada día me libro de una cosa por lo menos porque no me gusta el desorden.
5. Ella siempre se queja de trabajar tanto.
6. Me maravillo de las personas que pueden bailar bien.
7. Estoy encargado/a de cocinar y (tú) estás encargado/a de servir las comidas.
8. Con frecuencia me olvido del nombre de una persona, pero nunca me olvido de la cara.
9. Debes alejarte de personas peligrosas.
10. Acabo de leer un artículo maravilloso en el periódico.
11. ¿No tenemos jugo de naranja? Me muero de (la) sed.
12. ¿Quién va a cuidar de tu casa la semana que viene?
13. Ellos hablan de mudarse a Omaha el año que viene.
14. No me gusta estar con él porque siempre habla mal de otras personas.
15. Hay personas que abusan de otros (de los demás) sin remordimiento.

ejercicio   II-3-6

1. Algunas personas persisten en hacer ejercicio aun cuando están enfermas.
2. María se complace en tocar la guitarra en las fiestas.
3. Primero pienso en la comida y después pienso en comer algo.
4. Cada día debemos reflexionar en algo bueno de este mundo.
5. A finales del mes, Marcos siempre se ve en un apuro.
6. Cuando llega la policía, el ladrón consiente en ir con ellos pacíficamente.
7. Las personas que chismean se meten en la vida de otras personas.
8. Juan y María quedan (convienen) en consultar a un psiquiatra.
9. Cada año quedo en donar dinero a la Sociedad de Cáncer.
10. No debes meterte en sus problemas.
11. No estoy pensando (pienso) en nada ahora.
12. Mi hermana nunca se molesta en llamar por teléfono.
13. Me intereso mucho en la política internacional.
14. Tardo una hora en conducir (manejar) al estadio de aquí.
15. Para hacer ejercicio, los niños montan en bicicleta.

ejercicio   II-3-7

1. Usualmente es muy tarde cuando me siento para estudiar.
2. Martha Stewart dice que muchas cosas en la basura sirven para decoraciones en la casa.
3. A: ¿Están listos/as para salir (irse)? B: Sí, estamos listos/as para salir (irnos).
4. Estamos para almorzar.
5. Quiero trabajar para otra compañía.
6. ¿Quieres quedarte para mirar las noticias conmigo?
7. Esta película no sirve para nada.
8. Cada enero muchas personas trabajan para perder peso.
9. Melissa necesita por lo menos dos horas para prepararse para una cita.
10. Bjorn se prepara para encontrar un nuevo trabajo porque trabaja para un verdadero bruto.

ejercicio   II-3-8

1. Harold se preocupa por perder los dientes y el pelo.
2. En Anna Karenina, Levin lucha siempre por hacer lo correcto.
3. El pueblo de Argentina no debe llorar por Evita.
4. Yo miro (me preocupo) mucho por ti.
5. Muchas personas se ofenden por el desperdicio de comida en los restaurantes.
6. Me muero por ver tu nuevo peinado.
7. En esta oficina, clasificamos todo por tamaño.
8. Usualmente un gimnasta termina por hacer algo espectacular.
9. Ellos siempre optan por nadar en el río.
10. Cuando tengo una elección entre dos películas, usualmente opto por la que tiene las mejores reseñas.
11. Laura se impacienta por mudarse a otra parte del país.
12. Muchos abogados abogan por una persona culpable.
13. Te damos (las) gracias por decirnos la verdad.
14. Yo siempre clasifico mis libros por orden alfabético.
15. Ella siempre vota por el candidato menos atractivo.